Jesus and

the Gospels

The Cassell Biblical Studies Series

SERIES EDITOR: STEVE MOYISE

The Cassell Biblical Studies Series is aimed at those taking a course of biblical studies. Developed for the use of those embarking on theological and ministerial education, it is equally helpful in local church situations, and for lay people confused by apparently conflicting approaches to the Scriptures.

Students of biblical studies today will encounter a diversity of interpretive positions. Their teachers will – inevitably – lean towards some positions in preference to others. This series offers an integrated approach to the Bible which recognizes this diversity, but helps readers to understand it, and to work towards some kind of unity within it.

This is an ecumenical series, written by Roman Catholics and Protestants. The writers are all professionally engaged in the teaching of biblical studies in theological and ministerial education. The books are the product of that experience, and it is the intention of the editor, Dr Steve Moyise, that their contents should be tested on this exacting audience.

TITLES ALREADY PUBLISHED:

An Introduction to Biblical Studies
Steve Moyise
Historical Israel: Biblical Israel
Mary E. Mills

FORTHCOMING TITLES INCLUDE:

The Pentateuch: A Story of Beginnings
Paula Gooder
An Introduction to the Study of Paul
David G. Horrell

Jesus and
the Gospels

CLIVE MARSH

STEVE MOYISE

CASSELL

Cassell

Wellington House, 125 Strand, London WC2R 0BB

307 Lexington Avenue, New York, NY 10017-6550

www.cassell.co.uk

Unless otherwise stated, Scripture quotations are taken from the *New Revised Standard Version* of the Bible, © 1989 by the Division of Christian Education of the National Council of the Churches of Christ in the USA. Used by permission, all rights reserved.

First published 1999

British Library Cataloguing-in-Publication Data
A catalogue record for this book is available from the British Library.

ISBN 0-304-70487-3

Designed by Geoff Green
Editorial and typesetting by AD Publishing Services
Printed and bound in Great Britain by
Biddles Ltd, Guildford and King's Lynn

Contents

1 Introduction   7
2 Mark's Gospel   14
3 Matthew's Gospel   26
4 Luke's Gospel   38
5 John's Gospel   50
6 Apocryphal gospels   63
7 Jesus: prophet of doom?   72
8 Jesus: witty word-spinner?   84
9 Jesus, Gospels and different interests   96
10 How Christology works: the Gospels in practice   108

Appendix   115
Further reading   119
Bibliography   120
Index   125

1

Introduction

Writing the story of Jesus should be quite straightforward. He lived in the geographical area known as Palestine in what is called by the Western calendar 'the first century'. There is quite a lot of evidence about his life, although like the material about any historical figure, it is not presented in neat and unadorned form. So even if historians need to work at it, we should be able to offer a sketch of his life. But readers of this book will be looking for more than just a sketch. They want to know what Jesus believed and thought. They want to know his actual words. They want to know whether he really did the sort of things the Bible says he did. And providing this is rather more difficult.

For one thing, writing about someone's life requires selectivity. Towards the end of John's Gospel, we read: 'Now Jesus did many other signs in the presence of his disciples, which are not written in this book. But these are written so that you may come to believe that Jesus is the Messiah, the Son of God, and that through believing you may have life in his name' (20:30–1). The author is not claiming to be neutral or to be giving a comprehensive account of Jesus' life. He has selected just those incidents that he thinks will persuade his readers to adopt the position he is advocating. In fact, as we shall see in Chapter 5, he has selected a different set of incidents to those in Matthew, Mark and Luke.

A life story is also written from a certain angle. Even though the subject is just one person, the accounts which can be written about that person are numerous. Sometimes that is due to new evidence becoming available (such as letters, a relative speaking up after a long silence, long-lost tapes, or government documents being released). But this is not likely to happen very often for someone who lived 2000 years ago, though some scholars believe the discovery in 1945 of the *Gospel of Thomas* is such an event. So writers may simply be offering a different slant on the person by emphasizing one particular aspect of their life.

For example, Mark's Gospel consists of sixteen chapters, of which the last six are concerned with the final week of Jesus' life. Indeed, Mark tells us absolutely nothing about his first thirty years. He clearly wasn't aiming to produce a balanced biography.

A third difficulty is suggested by the name we give to our main sources. They are Gospels, accounts of the good news 'fulfilled among us' (Luke 1:1). Their aim is not simply to pass on historical data but to proclaim the *evangelion* (gospel). Thus Mark begins his account with the words, 'The beginning of the good news of Jesus Christ, the Son of God.' Christians claim that the historical Jesus of Nazareth was 'the Messiah', 'the Saviour', 'the Lord', or even 'God'. Such claims naturally affect the way that evidence is handled. For example, those who hold such views are more likely to accept the miraculous element in the Gospels than those who do not. But it is not just a matter of what one will accept or reject. It also affects the sort of questions one will ask. For example, no one seriously doubts that Jesus was crucified. But the statement 'Christ died for our sins' (1 Cor 15:3) is a rather different sort of judgement. Historians cannot pronounce on that but they can ask whether such a view was suggested by Jesus or is the product of later Christian reflection.

So writing a definitive 'life of Jesus' is far from straightforward. Readers who want to get at 'the historical Jesus', regardless of what Christians have made of him, may feel that faith keeps getting in the way. But that is unavoidable. It is, after all, what the Gospels are aiming to produce. On the other hand, Christian readers who only dabble in historical enquiry may be unhappy at what they see being done to the Gospels in the name of history. For historical study is about testing sources, comparing different versions of events and reconstructing the most likely scenario that explains the evidence. In particular, it will try not to say more than what the evidence allows (for an introduction to the historical study of the Bible, see the first volume in this series). But if Christian faith is linked closely to a historical figure, then it is difficult to dispute that such rigorous examination of texts is necessary. This book, therefore, deals throughout with matters of faith *and* history. The Gospels themselves link the two. Responsible reading of them requires that we carry on the struggle to clarify how the two are related.

The popularity of Jesus

In preparing this book, a quick Internet search with a major online bookstore revealed 799 titles about Jesus currently in print. So Jesus is clearly not someone to be confined to the church's understandings of him, even though it is through Christianity's careful preservation of four interpretations of his life and significance (Matthew, Mark, Luke and John) that so much about him is known. The impact of Jesus' sacrificial lifestyle, his commitment to a cause, his provocative teaching, his horrific death, his ability to relate to a wide cross-section of people – including those at the bottom of the social ladder – have all been cited as reasons why he has had such an impact. Sometimes people resist what has been made of Jesus (in the church, in the media, in departments of theology). But the historical figure of Jesus continues to be of great interest.

We shall, however, need to examine how that influence occurs. Is it just the 'historical Jesus' who has that impact? Or is it the particular 'image' or 'picture' of Jesus that was being propagated at the time? History tends to support the latter view, for it is easily demonstrated that books about Jesus in the nineteenth century were very different from those produced in the Middle Ages or the first few centuries. Furthermore, even within one particular historical period there are many 'images' of Jesus. These images differ because of the variety of influences on people's thinking and believing. For example, people's image of Jesus today may derive from the Bible, a particular church tradition, films about Jesus, documentaries, study courses, stained-glass windows, and religious art. Thus when we refer to 'Jesus and the Gospels', we are not simply speaking about the Jesus of history (Jesus as he was). We are also speaking about the particular 'images' of Jesus that are conveyed by these texts.

One Jesus, many gospels

But what are we to do with the fact that so *many* images of Jesus exist? In this book, we cannot deal with the thousands of images of Jesus made throughout Christian history, in art and on film as well as in words. (Those wishing to explore this fascinating aspect of Christian history should look at Jaroslav Pelikan's excellent book *Jesus Through the Centuries*, 1985, now available in an extensively illustrated version, 1997.) But even in Christian orthodoxy from earliest times, there have been a number of images of Jesus. Irenaeus (*c.* 200 CE) drew an analogy with the four living creatures of Revelation 4:6–7, suggesting that John's Gospel is like a lion, Luke's like a calf, Matthew's like a human being and Mark's like an eagle (see Appendix). As Richard Burridge notes, this was probably no more than applying the order of the creatures to the order of the Gospels as Irenaeus knew them (1994, pp. 23–32). But it does show that each of the Gospels was seen to offer a different image or portrait of Jesus.

However, the task is still to interpret the one Jesus. So we should not overplay this apparent diversity too much. No matter how many biographies and studies of the life and work of John F. Kennedy there are (and yet may be), there was still only one JFK. It is important, though, not to pinpoint too easily or quickly where the 'definitive' portrayal of a person is to be found. As far as Christian faith is concerned, the four Gospels, when read in the light of the later creeds (especially the Nicene and Apostles' Creeds), are certainly 'official and definitive' in their reading of Jesus. But the church is a fallible institution, and its conclusions must always be open to question. If it is claimed that the church's conclusions about Jesus somehow transcend all possibility of human error, then we need to be aware of the kind of judgement being made (i.e. God enabled Christians at one particular point in history to speak or write infallibly).

So although there is one Jesus there will always be many interpretations of him. Not all of them will be from a faith perspective, but all must deal with faith interpretations (Gospels), even if they dispense with some of the interpretations the Gospels offer (e.g. that Jesus is the Son of God). But because there is one Jesus, and he actually lived, then not every suggestion of what he was like will be equally plausible. It is possible, for example, to deny that Jesus was Jewish (and some have wished to do so, with disastrous consequences), yet all the evidence suggests that he was Jewish and all serious historians regard it as a fact. So any interpretation, whether constructed in faith or not, has to deal with that aspect of Jesus' life.

Of course, not all 'facts' about Jesus' life are quite so clear cut. Indeed, as we shall see, the number of 'facts' which receive widespread agreement is not large. But then indisputable facts are not the whole story. If from the first, history and faith were intertwined, then something more than 'facts' is being called for. Facts are not to be dispensed with. But the Gospels do not set out to present 'facts' alone. Indeed, even historians deal with more than just 'facts'. Events that seem highly probable must be linked with some imaginative, interpretative leaps ('if this, this and this happened, then it *must have been* because of this and that'). And given that Gospel writers and believers are not simply historians, our enquiry will prove an exciting and challenging one.

This world or the next?

Many scholars (e.g. Wright, 1996) have suggested that modern presentations of Jesus can be divided into two main categories. Either Jesus was a prophet of the end-time, who expected the world to pass away soon, probably in his own lifetime; or he was a wise teacher, a teller of tales and a spinner of pithy sayings, who was more interested in what happens in this world than in speculating about the next. Both of these images, as we shall see in later chapters, are firmly grounded in the Gospels, and some readers will conclude from this that they simply must be combined. It might even be suggested that keeping them apart is just a way of keeping scholars of both camps in paid employment! But the scholarly debate has a crucial point to it, for history is never undertaken for no purpose. If Jesus thought the end of the world was coming soon (see Mark 1:15; 9:1; 13:30), he was wrong. And this has implications for how he is to be regarded.

It is often assumed that the interpretation of Jesus as prophet of the end-time is somehow more Jewish, whereas the interpretation of Jesus as a wise teacher takes his Jewish origins less seriously. But this is not strictly true. Both are attempts to locate Jesus in his own time, and both try to clarify what kind of Jew he was and how he related to other first-century Jews. As we shall discover, it may seem easier to note the points of contact between the eschatological, prophetic tradition and the words and actions of Jesus. But this does not inevitably mean that Jesus must have been of that tradition.

One other feature common to both interpretations is worth noting. They each make considerable use of the extensive historical research into the social, political and economic conditions of first-century Palestine. In the past, such data has featured rather less than it should, probably because of the doctrinal framework (i.e. faith perspective) within which so much enquiry into the person of Jesus was undertaken. Currently, the work undertaken by Sean Freyne (1988) and Richard Horsley (1987) on the region of Galilee, and by Douglas Oakman (1986) into the first-century Palestinian economy, is especially significant.

Other interpretations of Jesus

However, not all scholars fit neatly into one or other of these two interpretations of Jesus (ironically, not even Wright himself). Thus Ben Witherington (1994) attempts to combine both tracks into a single interpretation (Jesus was both an eschatological prophet and a wisdom teacher). Jon Sobrino (1978) approaches the task from a 'liberation theology' perspective, challenging the Western emphasis on abstract doctrine. And Elisabeth Schüssler Fiorenza (1983) offers a feminist reading of Jesus, emphasizing the way in which the *basileia* (kingdom of God) was embodied within the community which Jesus formed around him. These variations show us that the 'two-track' approach is only an approximation. But it is undoubtedly helpful as a way of understanding the two main strands which intertwine within the theologically interpreted life-stories of Jesus, which we call Gospels.

But that is only the scholars. Something also should be said about what people make of Jesus beyond the world of scholarship. Undoubtedly the image of Jesus as inspiring teacher is prevalent inside and outside Christianity. Within churches, though, other images gain prominence. Jesus the miracle-worker is especially emphasized as a counterpart to the belief in God's capacity to transcend the natural conditions of the world. Indeed, the miracles of Jesus have been re-examined in recent scholarship (Meier, Theissen, Twelftree). Unlike so much historical enquiry from the late nineteenth and early twentieth centuries, which tended to assume that it had to explain away the miracle-stories in the Gospels, these studies show how the miracles are to be interpreted from out of their own first-century context. Without such studies, the image of Jesus as miracle-worker can too easily lead to assumptions about Jesus which begin to lose sight of his humanity. Popular interpretations of Jesus are, in other words, often prone to be 'docetic' (i.e. they suggest that Jesus was 'really' God and only 'appeared' to be human). But images of Jesus from beyond the world of scholarship are nevertheless important in drawing attention to what scholars might miss, or feel inclined to 'explain away'.

Beginning where we are

Before drawing this introductory chapter to a close, we must consider one further aspect of the way we interpret: the communities of inter-pretation out of which we approach the figure of Jesus. Of the various methods that have been used to study the Gospels, form and redaction criticism have taken pride of place (Moyise, 1998, pp. 33–48). Form criticism was based on the observation that the Gospels are like 'strings of pearls'. The individual units of tradition (*pericopae*) have been 'strung' together with simple phrases like 'after this' and 'one Sabbath'. Attention therefore focused on the individual units (parables, miracles, controversy stories, speeches) and how they might have been modified in transmission. Form critics were interested in two things: discovering the earliest form of a tradition, and learning about the communities that preserved them. Its weakness was that the Evangelists became little more than compilers supplying the 'cement' to bind the units together.

Redaction criticism aimed to correct this by focusing on the contri-bution of the Evangelists. This in turn led to an interest in the commu-nities to which they were writing. Why did Mark feel he had to emphasize the suffering of Jesus? Why did Matthew feel he had to emphasize the Jewishness of Jesus? Answers varied (as we shall see) but knowing *why* someone wrote (their context) is an important factor in understanding *what* they wrote.

More recently, scholars have awoken to the fact that the same is true of interpreters. Any interpreter of Jesus, any reader of Gospels, reads and interprets in a particular setting within a community (or range of communities). If I am a Christian, I shall be reading the Gospels within a church setting (even if not only there). If I am a student of religion, I shall be reading in an academic context (and I may be reading alongside psychologists, sociologists, historians or theologians). I may be reading this book for my own interest outside of both of those settings, but doing so because I think the Bible is important (culturally or morally) or because I want some more information about Jesus. Even this seemingly individual intent locates me within a particular 'reading community'. I will have political views, an economic status, a racial background and a sexual orientation, all of which locate me within particular groups of people which affect the way I read the Gospels and interpret the person of Jesus. There is no escaping this, and there should be no attempt to do so. Thus the historical figure can never be 'the historical Jesus' alone. He always reflects something of the communities by which he is interpreted. He should never be reduced to their needs. But he would not be considered at all if he were not relevant to those needs.

We therefore invite readers, before embarking on their own encounter with the Gospel texts themselves, and then with a range of ways in which the Gospels have been studied in the search for the figure of Jesus, to reflect on the communities out of which they read. At least they will then be more clear about some of the reasons why they react to the Gospels in the way they do. And it will be more possible for a creative conversation to take place between reader, Gospels, and the interpretations of Jesus which exist. After such reflection, reading Chapters 2 to 10 of this book should prove even more fruitful.

2

Mark's Gospel

Mark is the shortest of the four Gospels, beginning at Jesus' baptism (nothing about his birth) and ending at the empty tomb (no resurrection appearances). For much of church history, it was thought to be an abbreviation of Matthew and hence less important. Over 600 of its 661 verses find a parallel in Matthew, and although early tradition suggests that Mark drew on the memories of Peter (see Appendix), the fact remains that it was not written by an apostle. This probably explains why so few commentaries were written on Mark in the early church and the book fell into neglect (Lightfoot, 1950, p. 2).

However, during the nineteenth century, scholars such as Lachmann (1835) and Holtzmann (1863) showed that the 'abbreviation' theory is untenable. For example, the story of the demoniac and the pigs (Matt 8:28–34) occupies seven verses in Matthew but Mark's account runs to twenty verses (Mark 5:1–20). The similarities between the Gospels, particularly their use of unusual Greek phrases, shows that the church was correct in seeing a relationship between them. But most scholars today believe that Matthew and Luke used Mark as one of their sources (Luke acknowledges that many have written before him). This would make Mark our earliest 'life of Jesus' and therefore of great importance.

The flow of Mark's story is relatively straightforward. At an undisclosed date (compare Luke 3:1), Jesus makes the journey to the River Jordan to be baptized by John. It turns out to be a pivotal moment in his life. The heavens are torn apart (*schizo*), the Spirit descends on him like a dove and a voice proclaims, 'You are my Son, whom I love; with you I am well pleased' (1:9–11). He is then led into the wilderness for 40 days, 'being tempted by Satan'. Mark does not include the three specific temptations that we find in Matthew and Luke. He only tells us (somewhat enigmatically) that 'he was with the wild beasts; and the angels waited on him'.

We are not told what happened next. Richard Bauckham (1998, pp. 147–71) thinks there was a period when John the Baptist and Jesus worked in close proximity (John 3:22–30) but Mark does not tell us this. He simply notes that after John was put in prison, Jesus came into Galilee and gathered disciples. From among these, twelve were specifically selected 'to be with him, and to be sent out to proclaim the message, and to have authority to cast out demons' (3:14–15). Only one such 'sending out' is actually described (6:7–12). For the most part, the disciples remain 'with' Jesus as he embarks on an itinerant ministry of teaching, healing and exorcism in and around Galilee (chapters 2–9).

In Mark 10:1, Jesus leaves Capernaum and makes his way to Jerusalem. He enters the city on a colt, retires for the night in Bethany and returns next morning, where there is a skirmish in the temple (11:12–19). Chapter 12 sees him in dispute with representatives of various Jewish groups. Chapter 13 is a long discourse predicting the destruction of the temple and, on some interpretations, the end of the world. Then comes the passion narrative. Jesus is anointed at Bethany, shares a final meal with the disciples, agonizes in the garden of Gethsemane and is arrested and put on trial (chapter 14). He is then taken to the Roman procurator to be questioned (15:1–15). Pilate finds him innocent but the crowd demand his crucifixion and Pilate consents. He is crucified and buried (15:21–47). The most reliable manuscripts then end with a brief description of the empty tomb (16:1–8), to which later copyists added resurrection stories (printed as a separate paragraph in modern Bibles), which have clearly been taken from the other Gospels.

Thus Mark presents Jesus' ministry in two parts. The first ten chapters describe an itinerant ministry in and around Galilee. The last six chapters concern the last week of his life ('the passion') in and around Jerusalem. Unlike Matthew and Luke, Mark does not tell us anything about a miraculous birth or a child prodigy. Mark begins with Jesus' baptism and moves rapidly to his death. Over a third of Mark's Gospel is devoted to the final week of his life, earning it the description of 'a passion narrative with an extended introduction'.

Many scholars have also noted a thematic division in the Gospel. The first eight chapters present Jesus as a man 'mighty in word and deed'. But the incident at Caesarea Philippi (8:27–30) seems to be a turning point. Jesus asks his disciples, 'Who do people say I am?' They reply with a variety of answers: John the Baptist; Elijah; a prophet. He then asks, 'But who do you say that I am?', to which Peter replies, 'You are the Messiah'. Then *he began to teach them* that the Son of Man must undergo great suffering, and be rejected by the elders, the chief priests, and the scribes, and be killed, and after three days rise again. He said all this quite openly. And Peter took him aside and began to rebuke him. But turning and looking at his disciples, he rebuked Peter and said, 'Get behind me, Satan! For you are setting your mind not on divine things but on human things.' He called the crowd with his disciples, and said to them, 'If any want to become my followers, let them deny themselves and take up their cross and follow me. For those who want to save their life will lose it, and those who lose their life for my sake, and for the sake of the gospel, will save it.' (8:31–35)

Though chapters 9–16 are not devoid of miracles (there are three), the emphasis is on Jesus' suffering. It is the focus of his teaching (9:30–2; 10:32–4; 12:1–12; 14:8; 14:18–25). And it is the climax of Mark's story (14:34; 14:65; 15:15–20; 15:34). As Gundry puts it: 'The basic problem of Marcan studies is how to fit together these apparently contradictory kinds of material in a way that makes sense of the book as a literary whole' (1993, p.2).

Miracles

Mark records thirteen specific healing miracles (including exorcisms) along with a number of summary statements such as 1:34 ('And he cured many who were sick with various diseases'). The crowds are *exeplessonto* ('amazed', 'astonished'), *exestesan* ('astounded', 'amazed') and in 5:42, *exestesan ekstasei megale* (literally, 'amazed with a great amazement'). The effect of the miracles is that Jesus' popularity knows no bounds. In the first chapter alone, we read:

1:28 'At once his fame began to spread throughout the surrounding region of Galilee.'
1:33 'And the whole city was gathered around the door.'
1:37 'When they found him, they said to him, "Everyone is searching for you."'
1:45 'And people came to him from every quarter.'

According to Theissen (1998, ch. 10), healing stories fall into a number of categories. Some are narrated in a fairly simple three-fold pattern: (a) the illness is described; (b) Jesus either says something or does something; and (c) the person is described as 'healed', 'restored' or 'cleansed'. For example, in Mark 1:30–1: (a) 'Now Simon's mother-in-law was in bed with a fever, and they told him about her at once'; (b) 'He came and took her by the hand and lifted her up'; (c) 'Then the fever left her, and she began to serve them.'

Other stories are more complex. For example, the story of the paralytic (2:1–12) and the man with the withered hand (3:1–6) are both interwoven with a dispute. In the first, the 'teachers of the law' regard Jesus' statement that the man's sins are forgiven as blasphemy. From then on, the healing appears to be subsidiary to the dispute. In the story of the man with the withered hand, the dispute is over whether it is right to heal on the Sabbath. This time the healing remains central but not before Jesus has outmanoeuvred his opponents.

As well as healing stories, Jesus is involved in some spectacular 'nature' miracles. For example, when the disciples are struggling against a sudden storm, Jesus stands up and orders the wind and the waves to be still (4:39). On another occasion, Jesus comes to the disciples by walking on water (6:48). And just before that, he miraculously feeds a crowd of 5000 from five loaves and two fishes (6:30–44). This is repeated in chapter 8, where seven loaves feed a crowd of 4000. Proportionately, Mark contains more miracles (which he calls *dynameis*, 'mighty works') than any of the other Gospels.

Teacher

As well as a miracle-worker, Mark presents Jesus as a great teacher. This is seen in at least three ways. First, Mark describes the effect of Jesus' teaching: 'They were astounded at his teaching, for he taught them as one having authority, and not as the scribes' (1:22). Secondly, Mark gives examples of Jesus confounding his opponents by his superior wisdom and insight. We have already mentioned two examples of this in the healing of the paralytic and the man with the withered hand. When Jesus arrives in Jerusalem, there are more overt examples: the paying of taxes to Caesar (12:13–17) and marriage and the resurrection (12:18-27).

Thirdly, Mark gives examples of his teaching, though these are relatively sparse compared with the other three Gospels (there is no sermon on the mount, good Samaritan or prodigal son parables, or even the Lord's Prayer). The two chapters that are particularly concerned with Jesus' teaching are chapter 4, with its collection of 'seed' parables (sower, seed growing secretly, mustard seed), and the apocalyptic discourse in chapter 13. Both appear to be about the kingdom of God. The first speaks of its mysterious growth and inevitable harvest, while the latter speaks of the persecutions and suffering that will precede the 'coming' of the Son of Man. The interpretation of this language has been a key feature in understanding Mark's portrait of Jesus. What was it that Jesus expected to happen?

Urgency

One of Mark's key words is *euthus* ('immediately'), used no less than 42 times in the Gospel. It emphasizes the immediacy of the impact Jesus had on people. For example, when he calls the fishermen, '*immediately* they left their nets and followed him' (1:18). When he gives the order for the leper to be clean, the leprosy *immediately* left him (1:42). When the teachers of the law think Jesus is blaspheming, he *immediately* knew what they were thinking (2:8). It is for this reason that the two-stage healing in Mark 8:22–26 stands out as exceptional. We have come to expect everything to happen *immediately*.

Moreover, given that Jesus comes into Galilee and proclaims, 'The time is fulfilled, and the kingdom of God has come near' (1:15), this urgency appears to be eschatological. Time is running out. He says to the disciples just before the transfiguration: 'Truly I tell you, there are some standing here who will not taste death until they see that the kingdom of God has come with power' (9:1). And at the conclusion of the apocalyptic discourse, we read: 'Truly I tell you, this generation will not pass away until all these things have taken place' (13:30). But to what is this referring? Albert Schweitzer thought it was an obvious reference to the end of the world, for what else can Mark 13:24–27 be referring to?

> The sun will be darkened, and the moon will not give its light, and the stars will be falling from heaven, and the powers in the heavens will be shaken. Then they will see 'the Son of Man coming in clouds' with great power and glory. Then he will send out the angels, and gather his elect from the four winds, from the ends of the earth to the ends of heaven.

Others have pointed out that if the sun and moon were darkened and the stars fell from the sky, there would be no one left to witness 'the Son of Man coming in clouds'. It is clearly figurative language. Indeed, the words come from Isaiah 13:10 and 34:4, where they refer to a historical judgement on Israel's enemies. The difference is that now these images are being used to describe a judgement on Israel, in which its temple will once again be destroyed (13:2: 'not one stone will be left here upon another; all will be thrown down'). It is clear then that Mark presents Jesus as expecting a cataclysmic event of some kind to happen soon. But there are differences of opinion as to whether this is the end of the world or the end of temple religion.

Conflict

Mark's Gospel is a story of conflict (Garrett, 1998). We have seen how Jesus' claim to forgive sins and willingness to heal on the Sabbath led to opposition from the religious authorities. This leads to a decision to kill Jesus as early as 3:6 (in Matthew, not until 12:14; in Luke, not until 19:47). There is further conflict in Mark 7, where his opponents accuse him of eating with 'unclean' hands. He replies by calling them hypocrites (7:6). In chapter 8, they come asking for a sign and are sent away with the words, 'Why does this generation ask for a sign? Truly I tell you, no sign will be given to this generation' (8:12). The next few chapters focus on Jesus teaching his disciples, but hostilities are resumed in chapter 11 where he 'cleanses' the temple. Once again, the religious leaders vow to kill Jesus (11:18) and set a number of traps. He is questioned over his authority (11:27–33), paying taxes (12:13–17), the status of marriage at the resurrection (12:18–27) and the greatest commandment (12:28–34). But these turn out to be opportunities for Jesus to demonstrate his superior wisdom. When their attempts fail, they arrange to have him arrested, tried before the Sanhedrin and handed over to Pilate. Even on the cross, people abuse him, along with the criminals on his left and right (only Luke has the penitent thief).

But behind this human conflict lies a supernatural conflict. As soon as Jesus is baptized, he is sent out into the desert. The word for 'sent out' is *ekballo*, the same word used for Jesus 'casting out' demons. Jesus is thrust out to do battle with Satan. We are not told the result but many scholars believe that Mark 3:20–30 provides the answer. Jesus has been accused of working miracles by being in league with the devil (Beelzebul). He refutes the suggestion by declaring that a divided kingdom cannot stand, a divided house cannot stand and a divided Satan cannot stand (3:24–6). He concludes that 'no one can enter a strong man's house and plunder his property without first tying up the strong man; then indeed the house can be plundered' (3:27). According to Kingsbury, this is the clue to Mark's understanding of Jesus' ministry. His exorcisms are signs that Satan's kingdom is being plundered:

> God impels Jesus, whom he has just declared to be his Son, into the desert to confront Satan in the place of his abode. For forty days Jesus, sustained by angels, is put to the test by Satan. But far from succumbing to Satan's assault, which would have alienated him from God, Jesus Son of God proves himself to be stronger than the 'strong man'. Thus, he overcomes Satan and 'binds' him, and so inaugurates the eschatological age of salvation. (1983, p. 69)

The paradox of Mark's Gospel

Most scholars believe the key to Mark's presentation lies in the way that 'glory' passages are juxtaposed with 'suffering' passages. For most of the first ten chapters, Jesus is a heroic figure, able to do whatever he likes. His wisdom astounds his hearers. His skill at debating humiliates his opponents. His power silences demons and heals people of their diseases. Yet when he faces death, he does not face it like heroes of the past nor of those of the future. Compare, for example, Mark's account of Jesus' death with Luke's account of Stephen's martyrdom:

Mark 15:34–7
At three o'clock Jesus cried out with a loud voice, 'Eloi, Eloi, lema sabachthani?' which means, 'My God, my God, why have you forsaken me?' When some of the bystanders heard it, they said, 'Listen, he is calling for Elijah.' And someone ran, filled a sponge with sour wine, put it on a stick, and gave it to him to drink, saying, 'Wait, let us see whether Elijah will come to take him down.' Then Jesus gave a loud cry and breathed his last.

Acts 7:58–60
Then they dragged him out of the city and began to stone him... While they were stoning Stephen, he prayed, 'Lord Jesus, receive my spirit.' Then he knelt down and cried out in a loud voice, 'Lord, do not hold this sin against them.' When he had said this, he died.

Jesus' cry of despair echoes the plea in the garden of Gethsemane, where he asks if there is some other way of doing God's will:

They went to a place called Gethsemane; and he said to his disciples, 'Sit here while I pray.' He took with him Peter and James and John, and began to be *distressed* and *agitated*. And he said to them, '*I am deeply grieved, even to death*; remain here, and keep awake.' And going a little farther, he *threw himself on the ground* and prayed that, if it were possible, the hour *might pass from him*. He said, 'Abba, Father, for you all things are possible; *remove this cup from me*; yet, not what I want, but what you want.' (14:32–6)

Paradox is also present in Jesus' teaching ministry, for who, in the end, has been convinced? The religious leaders oppose him and have him killed. The crowds, who were amazed and astounded, call for his crucifixion (15:6–14). The people he grew up with take offence at him (6:3) and his own family think he is mad (3:21). This leaves the disciples, those specially chosen by Jesus to be with him. At the close of the parables chapter, Mark tells us that while parables are for outsiders, 'he explained everything in private to his disciples' (4:34). In chapters 8–10, Jesus withdraws from the crowds so as to teach the disciples (see especially 9:31). Among the disciples, Peter, James and John are singled out for special instruction and allowed to witness the raising of Jairus' daughter (5:37) and the transfiguration (9:2).

But how much have they grasped? They are rebuked for arguing over who is to be the greatest (9:33), for trying to stop a fellow exorcist (9:39), for forbidding children to come to Jesus (10:14), for criticising the woman who anoints him (14:6) and for falling asleep in Gethsemane (14:37). Jesus criticizes their lack of faith in the two boat incidents (4:40; 6:50). He is amazed at their lack of understanding over a parable (7:18), and if Jesus says that the crowds have eyes but never see and ears that never hear in 4:12, he says the same of the disciples in 8:18. The greatest teacher that ever lived has been unable to convince anyone as to his true nature and mission.

Mark therefore presents us with a paradox. The most powerful man who ever lived died in despair, wishing that there was some other way of doing God's will. The most amazing teacher who ever lived is unable to impart understanding even to his closest disciples. Any interpretation of Mark must do justice to these two elements. In particular, it must offer a rationale for why Mark leaves us with such a paradox. The following are the main suggestions that have been offered.

No Christianity without the cross

The majority view is that Mark intended to show that there can be no glory without the cross. As Paul discovered, God's glory is not revealed in strength but weakness. The burden of Mark's Gospel is to show that even with his mighty power and superior wisdom, Jesus could only accomplish his work through suffering. The same will be true for his followers. To an earlier generation of scholars (Taylor, 1953; Cranfield, 1959), this was seen as Jesus fusing together the glorious 'Son of Man' figure from Daniel 7 with the suffering servant of Isaiah 53. This is a rather neat solution, but it is probably too neat. There is little evidence that Jews of Jesus' day were expecting a messianic 'Son of Man' or a 'suffering servant'. And there are no actual quotations of Isaiah 53 in Mark's Gospel. The three quotations that do appear in connection with Jesus' death are Psalm 118:22–3 ('The stone that the builders rejected'), Zechariah 13:7 ('I will strike the shepherd, and the sheep will be scattered') and Psalm 22:1 ('My God, my God, why have you forsaken me?'). As Joel Marcus has shown, Mark seems to have drawn on a number of Old Testament figures in order to paint his picture of Jesus' passion (1992, pp. 153–98).

Many have suggested that Mark is writing at a time of extreme tension, either the Neronian persecution in Rome (c. 64 CE) or, more probably (in the light of 13:14), the Jewish war (c. 66–70 CE). It is often thought of as the 'suffering' Gospel. Thus Denis Nineham (1963, p. 33) thinks that the author of Mark's Gospel had three aims:

- to show how much Jesus suffered
- to show how he taught his followers that they would suffer
- to show how he promised great rewards to those who endure to the end.

The crucified Jesus is the Son of God

Robert Gundry (1993) reverses this. He believes that the readers are well aware that Jesus suffered and was crucified. Every time they attempt to preach the gospel they are reminded that Jesus was a convicted criminal who died an ignominious death. They do not need reminding that Jesus suffered and died. But they do need reminding that Jesus was the Son of God, who won for them a powerful victory. This is what Peter preached at Pentecost:

> Jesus of Nazareth, a man attested to you by God with deeds of power, wonders, and signs that God did through him among you... this man, handed over to you according to the definite plan and foreknowledge of God, you crucified and killed by the hands of those outside the law. But God raised him up, having freed him from death, because it was impossible for him to be held in its power. (Acts 2:22-4)

Gundry accepts the ancient tradition that Mark was the interpreter of Peter (see Appendix) and thus sees a link with Peter's sermon. Mark aims to show how the 'man attested to you by God with deeds of power' was crucified 'according to the definite plan and foreknowledge of God'. Thus the Gospel opens with the words, 'The beginning of the good news of Jesus Christ, the Son of God.' And it comes to a close when a centurion declares, 'Truly this man was God's Son!' (15:39). If the disciples in the story find this hard to understand, this does not shake the readers' belief for they hear God declaring it at his baptism (1:11) and transfiguration (9:7). Thus, according to Gundry, Mark is not trying to show that all this needs 'correcting' by a theology of suffering. Rather, he shows by means of the passion predictions, the torn curtain and the empty tomb, that Jesus' crucifixion was really a mighty victory. Indeed, Gundry thinks that it was the power of Jesus' final cry that tore the temple curtain.

A non-messianic Jesus

In 1901, William Wrede published his famous book on the 'messianic secret'. Prior to this, it was assumed that Jesus wanted people to know who he was and why he had come. Why else would God become incarnate if not to try and communicate with lost humanity? But Mark portrays Jesus as frequently *commanding* silence from those who are healed and *refusing* to work miracles to aid belief:

1:34   The demons are forbidden to say who Jesus is (see also 3:12).
1:44   The leprosy sufferer is told to tell no one about his cure.
5:43   Jairus is told to tell no one about the raising of his daughter.
7:36   The crowd must not tell of the healing of the deaf mute.
9:9   Peter, James and John are not to tell anyone about the transfiguration.
9:30   Jesus wants to keep his presence a secret.

Wrede, about whom we shall have more to say in Chapter 8, believed that these are unrealistic and artificial. How could Jairus say nothing about the raising of his daughter when there is a crowd of mourners outside? And if Jesus is seeking to avoid attention, why does he insist on healing the man with the withered hand in the middle of a synagogue service? Why not wait until the next day? Why does he feed a crowd of 5000 if he wants to remain anonymous? Wrede concluded that this is really a literary device to cover up the fact that while the church proclaimed Jesus as Messiah, Jesus himself had no such pretensions. In order to get around this, the church introduced the 'messianic secret', the idea that Jesus knew himself to be the Messiah but wished to keep it quiet. But actually, Jesus was not conscious of being the Messiah and never made any such claims.

A non-political Messiah

Conservative scholars interpret this evidence differently. Jesus knew that he was the Messiah and Son of God (e.g. 13:32) but did not openly proclaim it, either for fear of creating sedition or of encouraging the wrong sort of faith (Cranfield, 1959, p. 270). He knew that groups like the Zealots would pounce on such claims and try to lead a revolt against Rome (as in fact they did *c.* 66–70 CE). So he veiled his teaching in parables. He spoke about the kingdom rather than proclaiming himself as king. He preferred to use the obscure 'Son of Man' (the Aramaic simply means 'human') rather than openly declaring himself to be the 'Messiah' or 'Son of God'. But when asked at his trial, 'Are you the Messiah, the Son of the Blessed One?', he answered, 'I am' (14:61–2).

At this stage, there was no longer any need to keep his true status quiet. Thus Wrede was correct in drawing attention to a key characteristic of Mark but had misinterpreted it. Peter is not rebuked for calling Jesus 'Messiah' but for his inability to see that the Messiah must suffer (8:32).

Son of Man and Son of God

Any interpretation of Mark must do justice both to the 'glory' passages and the 'suffering' passages. In terms of Mark's Christology, this has often been discussed with respect to his use of the titles 'Son of God' and 'Son of Man'. The distribution of these titles is curious, for 'Son of Man' appears to be Jesus' preferred title (fourteen times), while Mark clearly wishes his readers to think of Jesus as 'Son of God' (1:1,11; 9:7; 12:6; 13:32; 15:39). This could be seen as a point in favour of Mark's reliability. Mark sees Jesus as Son of God but he does not make Jesus a mouthpiece for his own theology. Rather, he presents Jesus as preferring 'Son of Man', even though the early church (according to Acts) seems to have ignored it.

On the other hand, Mark presents Jesus as using 'Son of Man' as a *title*, whereas the Aramaic phrase simply means 'a human being', sometimes with a self-reference ('one such as I'). This sounds odd at first but there is evidence in the Gospels that 'I' and 'Son of Man' are interchangeable:

Matthew 10:32	*Luke 12:8*
Everyone therefore who acknowledges me before others, *I* also will acknowledge before my Father in heaven.	And I tell you, everyone who acknowledges me before others, the *Son of Man* also will acknowledge before the angels of God.

Did Jesus use the phrase as a self-reference ('one such as I'), which was only taken as a title when the Aramaic was translated into Greek (the form of the Greek is definitely a title)? It would certainly clarify Mark 9:12 ('How then is it written about the Son of Man, that he is to go through many sufferings...?'), since there are no Old Testament texts which predict a suffering 'Son of Man'. But in Aramaic, the saying would simply mean, 'How then is it written about "one such as I", that he is to go through many sufferings...?' It is also a plausible understanding of most of the other sayings in Mark:

2:10 But so that you may know that 'one such as I' has authority on earth to forgive sins.

2:27f The sabbath was made for humankind, and not humankind for the sabbath; so 'one such as I' is lord even of the sabbath.

10:33 See, we are going up to Jerusalem, and 'one such as I' will be handed over to the chief priests.

13:26 Then they will see 'one such as I' coming in clouds with great power and glory.

14:62 You will see 'one such as I' seated at the right hand of the Power.

Those who dispute this interpretation do so on the grounds that 13:26 and 14:62 are probably allusions to Daniel 7, which speaks of 'one like a son of man' receiving 'glory and kingship' and an 'everlasting dominion that shall not pass away' (Dan 7:14). Jesus, it is maintained, is not just saying 'one such as I' but is claiming to be the exalted figure in Daniel's vision. But the two views are not mutually exclusive. Daniel's vision contrasts the four beasts, which represent evil empires, with 'one like a son of man' (NRSV: 'one like a human being'), who receives an everlasting kingdom. But when Daniel asks for an interpretation of the vision, he is told that 'the holy ones of the Most High shall receive the kingdom and possess the kingdom for ever' (7:18). Jesus may not be saying, 'I am the Son of Man', as if this were an expected figure like 'Messiah' ('riding on the clouds'). But he may be alluding to the whole scenario of Daniel 7, in order to express his hope that his obedience unto death will be vindicated by God (Hooker, 1967, pp. 174–98).

Conclusion

The early church believed that Mark was an abbreviation of Matthew and so the book fell into neglect. But most scholars today (Farmer is an exception) believe that Mark is the earliest Gospel and therefore of great importance. In particular, its candid portrayal of a suffering, forsaken Jesus (and the many failures of the disciples) has resonated powerfully with post-war readers (Moltmann, 1974). More recently, the paradoxical nature of the Gospel (on some readings) has appealed to what many have called our postmodern world. Far from providing 'answers', Aichele deduces from the Gospel's abrupt ending that Mark

is not a story which ends happily or comfortably for readers who want the reinforcing of Christian faith. It does not end with a meeting between the disciples and the resurrected Jesus, nor with Jesus seated on the right hand of God. It does not end with an imperishable message of everlasting salvation spreading out from east to west, nor with the end of the reign of Satan, nor with a promise of heavenly glory, nor with Jesus transformed, nor with transformed disciples. (1996, p. 51)

For such things, we have to look to the other Gospels and the rest of the New Testament.

3

Matthew's Gospel

Since Matthew contains over 90 per cent of Mark, one might assume that its picture of Jesus is essentially the same. There is, for example, the same juxtaposition of powerful miracle-worker and suffering death. Matthew includes all but two of Mark's miracle stories and Jesus' only words from the cross are, 'My God, my God, why have you forsaken me?' (27:46). He also follows Mark's structure of a Galilean ministry, which reaches a climax in Peter's confession, followed by a final week in Jerusalem. The Galilean ministry begins with the same sense of urgency ('Repent, for the kingdom of heaven has come near') and there is a similar conflict with demons and religious leaders.

However, Matthew differs from Mark in at least four significant ways. First, he includes two chapters of infancy stories. Mark tells us nothing about Jesus' birth or early life. Matthew begins with a genealogy, which traces Jesus' lineage back to Abraham. He then tells us of the miraculous conception of Jesus, the visit of the magi, the flight to Egypt and the subsequent settling in a town called Nazareth. Mark could be interpreted as meaning that Jesus was an ordinary man until his experience of God at his baptism. Matthew makes it clear that God was involved in his life from the very moment of conception. Indeed, his conception was a work of the Holy Spirit (1:18).

Secondly, Matthew presents Jesus' teaching in five major blocks or discourses (chapters 5–7, 10, 13, 18, 24–5). The first of these is usually called the 'sermon on the mount'. This is where we find the beatitudes ('Blessed are the poor in spirit/those who mourn/the meek'), the Lord's Prayer and the parable of the wise and foolish builders. Chapter 10 appears to be an expansion of Mark's sending out of the twelve (Mark 6:7–12), with additional teaching on discipleship and persecution (Matt 10:17–42). Mark's collection of 'seed' parables (Mark 4:1–34) is expanded to include the parables of the 'wheat and tares', 'hidden treasure', 'costly pearl' and 'net' (Matt 13:24–52). Matthew 18 begins with the saying about receiving the kingdom like a child (Mark 10:15) but leads into a discourse about relationships within the church. And Matthew 24–5 contains an expansion of Mark's apocalyptic discourse (Mark 13:5–37), which now ends with a sequence of parables ('faithful servant', 'ten virgins', 'talents', 'sheep and goats').

Thirdly, Matthew narrates a reunion between Jesus and the disciples in Galilee (28:16–20). We do not know whether Mark intended to end his Gospel abruptly for theological reasons or if the original ending was lost, but Matthew differs from our earliest manuscripts of Mark in that he provides a 'happy' ending. The women overcome their fear and set out to tell the disciples about the empty tomb. On the way, the risen Jesus appears to them and 'they took hold of his feet, and worshipped him' (28:9). Then Matthew describes the reunion of Jesus and the disciples in Galilee where they too 'worshipped him; but some doubted' (28:17). The Gospel ends with the triumphant commission to go and 'make disciples of all nations, baptizing them in the name of the Father and of the Son and of the Holy Spirit, and teaching them to obey everything that I have commanded you' (28:19–20).

Fourthly, there are a number of differences between Matthew and Mark when they each tell the same story. Most scholars believe these to be Matthew's changes to Mark, though it has to be said that it is difficult to find a consistent rationale that explains them all. For example, many of Matthew's stories are shorter than the parallel in Mark but that is not true of the temptation narrative, in which Matthew includes three specific temptations. Some of Mark's secrecy sayings have gone, but not all of them. If Matthew was unhappy with this element of Mark, why did he not remove them all? We shall now look at each of these four areas of difference in more detail.

Infancy stories (chapters 1–2)

Mark opens his Gospel with the words, 'The beginning of the good news of Jesus Christ, the Son of God.' Matthew begins, 'An account of the genealogy of Jesus the Messiah, the son of David, the son of Abraham.' It is evident from this that Matthew wishes to tie the story of Jesus far more closely to Jewish history than Mark. The opening words in Greek are *biblos geneseos* ('book of origins'), which links Matthew's story with God's creative acts at the very beginning (Gen 2:4; 5:1). Mark tells us that Jesus is 'Son of God' which Matthew will affirm elsewhere, but here he emphasizes Jesus' continuity with David, king of Israel, and Abraham, the father of Israel. It is probably for this reason that the NRSV has chosen to translate *christos* as 'Messiah' in Matthew 1:1 but 'Christ' in Mark 1:1 (virtually as a surname).

Also of note in this very Jewish opening is the fact that the genealogy mentions three women by name (Tamar, Rahab, Ruth), all of whom are Gentile or have Gentile connections. Several suggestions have been offered for this. It could be that it anticipates the admission of Gentiles into the people of God (Matt 28:19–20). Or it might anticipate the role of Mary in the birth of Jesus, though Matthew's emphasis is more on Joseph. A third possibility is that Matthew is making a more general point about God, who uses people from all walks of life to fulfil his purposes.

Many readers will know the infancy stories through nativity plays where Matthew, Luke and a little imagination are combined. Matthew's account does not actually describe the birth of Christ. It simply tells us that Joseph 'had no marital relations with [Mary] until she had borne a son', that this son was named Jesus, and that this happened in the time of King Herod (1:24 – 2:1). What Matthew does emphasize is the way that these events are a fulfilment of scripture:

All this took place to fulfil what had been spoken by the Lord through the prophet: 'Look, the virgin shall conceive and bear a son, and they shall name him Emmanuel', which means, 'God is with us.' (1:22–3; cf. Isa 7:14)

They told him, 'In Bethlehem of Judea; for so it has been written by the prophet: "And you, Bethlehem, in the land of Judah, are by no means least among the rulers of Judah; for from you shall come a ruler who is to shepherd my people Israel."' (2:5; cf. Mic 5:2)

Then Joseph got up, took the child and his mother by night, and went to Egypt, and remained there until the death of Herod. This was to fulfil what had been spoken by the Lord through the prophet, 'Out of Egypt I have called my son.' (2:14–15; cf. Hos 11:1)

Herod... killed all the children in and around Bethlehem who were two years old or under, according to the time that he had learned from the wise men. Then was fulfilled what had been spoken through the prophet Jeremiah: 'A voice was heard in Ramah, wailing and loud lamentation, Rachel weeping for her children; she refused to be consoled, because they are no more.' (2:16–18; cf. Jer 31:15)

There he made his home in a town called Nazareth, so that what had been spoken through the prophets might be fulfilled, 'He will be called a Nazorean.' (2:23; source unknown)

Study of these and the many other quotations in Matthew has led some scholars to the conclusion that the author is a converted Jewish scribe and that the Gospel is the product of a school of interpretation.

Krister Stendahl (1968), for example, draws parallels with the Dead Sea Scrolls. These were the product of a community engaged in scripture study, intent on showing that the ancient prophecies were coming true in their own history. To do this, they used a number of interpretative techniques. For example, scripture was known in a variety of Hebrew, Aramaic and Greek manuscripts. This was exploited by the Qumran interpreters by choosing the reading that best supported the author's point. Matthew does the same when he quotes Isaiah 7:14, not according to the Hebrew, which speaks of a young woman (*almah*) conceiving, but a Greek translation which used the word 'virgin' (*parthenos*).

Another technique was to change the actual wording of the quotation in order to clarify its true meaning (in the eyes of the interpreter). In Matthew's quotation of Micah 5:2, both the Hebrew and the Greek say that Bethlehem *is* the least among the rulers of Judah but Matthew has inserted the word *oudamos* ('by no means'), effectively reversing the meaning ('*by no means* least among the rulers of Judah'). The aim is not deception. The readers know what the original quotation says. Rather, it is a way of making the point that now that Jesus *has* arisen from Bethlehem, it will *no longer* be considered least among the rulers. Modern exegesis would prefer to make the point in two stages. It would first quote the text accurately and then point out that an ironic reversal has taken place. But first-century exegesis was happy to combine these in a single modified quotation.

If Stendahl is correct, then it is hard to believe that the author is a tax-collector, as Christian tradition has maintained (see Appendix). Indeed, the question of the authorship of the Gospel appears confused from the very beginning. In Mark 2:14, the tax-collector is called 'Levi son of Alphaeus' and does not appear in the list of the twelve (though there is a James, son of Alphaeus in Mark 3:18). In Matthew's Gospel, the tax-collector is now called Matthew and does appear in the list of the twelve (Matt 9:9; 10:4). Now our two earliest witnesses to the authorship of the Gospels are Papias (*c.* 130 CE) and Irenaeus (*c.* 180 CE), who both speak of Matthew as recording 'the sayings' (Papias) or 'his gospel' (Irenaeus) in the Hebrew tongue (see Appendix). Irenaeus adds that this was when 'Peter and Paul were preaching the gospel in Rome and founding the church there'.

Several questions arise from this testimony, however. First, did they have actual evidence for this view or were they simply making a deduction from the change in the name of the tax-collector? Secondly, both claim that Matthew wrote in the Hebrew tongue but the Gospel, as we have it, was certainly composed in Greek. Indeed, the majority of scholars believe that the author used the Greek text of Mark as one of his sources. Thirdly, what does Papias mean by 'the sayings'? This could be referring to a collection of Jesus' sayings rather than to what we know as Matthew's Gospel. And fourthly, when were Peter and Paul founding the church in Rome? It is clear from Paul's letter to the Romans (c. 55 CE) that he is not the founder of that church (Rom 1:8–13). Does Irenaeus mean 'establishing' rather than 'founding'? Or is this simply a second-century defence of the pre-eminence of the Roman church and the apostolic authorship of the four Gospels? Most scholars today accept that the author, who is not named in the Gospel, must remain anonymous, though the traditional view still has its supporters (e.g. France, 1989).

The five discourses (chapters 5–7, 10, 13, 18, 24–5)

Each of the five discourses ends with a formula like 'when he had finished these sayings' (7:28; 11:1; 13:53; 19:1; 26:1), which suggests a deliberate plan to interweave narrative and discourse. Furthermore, from the length of these discourses and their position in the Gospel, it also looks like the author had an eye for symmetry:

Chapter(s)	Theme	
5-7	Discourse on righteousness	(109 verses)
10	Discourse on missionary work	(42 verses)
13	Discourse on the kingdom	(52 verses)
18	Discourse on the church	(35 verses)
24–5	Discourse on things to come	(97 verses)

Since this is a sizeable collection of teaching, one might ask where this material came from and what sort of picture of Jesus it offers. One suggestion is that when Papias says that Matthew 'compiled the *Sayings* in the Aramaic language', he is not referring to the written Gospel but to an earlier 'sayings' source. If this is correct, then it could be that Matthew's Gospel draws on a tradition that goes back to the tax-collector and a tradition that goes back to Peter (i.e. Mark). This would be a neat solution to the authorship question but is no more than a speculation.

So what picture emerges from this material? Clearly it portrays Jesus as a great teacher. One of the intriguing aspects of Mark is that while it tells us that Jesus taught with authority, it does not actually tell us much about what he taught. This is remedied in Matthew, where Jesus delivers his teaching in five great blocks, just as the Psalms and the Torah are each divided into five books. Bacon (1930) focused on the latter and argued that Matthew presents Jesus as a new Moses, bringing a new law to God's people. Thus Jesus delivers his great discourse on righteousness from a mountain and specifically links his teaching with that of Moses ('You have heard... But I say to you' – 5:21,27,31,33,38, 43). There are many similarities in their birth stories, notably the 'slaughter of the innocents' (Matt 2:16–18; Exod 1:15–22) and the mention of Egypt. And when Jesus ascends the Mount of Transfiguration, his face shines, as did the face of Moses at Mount Sinai (Exod 34:29–35). Further parallels can be found in Dale Allison's excellent study, *The New Moses: A Matthean Typology* (1993).

Others have drawn attention to the 'wisdom' nature of Jesus' teaching. Far from issuing threats about the end of the world, much of this material focuses on a particular type of lifestyle. Burton Mack (1997, pp. 32–3) believes that Matthew has taken this from the sayings source commonly called Q, which according to his summary is akin to that of a wandering Cynic philosopher:

- a criticism of the rich and their wealth
- a critique of hypocrisy and pretension
- fearlessness in the presence of those in power and authority
- a challenge to renounce the supports usually considered necessary for human life
- a call to voluntary poverty
- a challenge to fearless and carefree attitudes
- etiquette for unashamed begging
- etiquette for responding to public reproach
- non-retaliation
- disentanglement from family ties
- a strong sense of independent vocation
- concern for personal integrity and authenticity
- a challenge to live naturally at any cost
- a reliance on the natural order
- singlemindedness in the pursuit of God's kingdom
- confidence in God's care.

The discourses on missionary work (chapter 10), the kingdom (chapter 13) and things to come (chapters 24–5) all have parallels in Mark. But the discourse on the church (chapter 18) stands out as a particular characteristic of Matthew. The promise to Peter in Matthew 16:19 that 'whatever you bind on earth will be bound in heaven, and whatever you loose on earth will be loosed in heaven' is extended to the church in 18:18. Immediately before that, we are told:

> If another member of the church (RSV: 'your brother') sins against you, go and point out the fault when the two of you are alone. If the member listens to you, you have regained that one. But if you are not listened to, take one or two others along with you, so that every word

may be confirmed by the evidence of two or three witnesses. If the member refuses to listen to them, tell it to the church (*ekklesia*); and if the offender refuses to listen even to the church (*ekklesia*), let such a one be to you as a Gentile and a tax-collector (18:15–17).

Appearances of the risen Jesus (chapter 28)

Unlike Mark's Gospel, which appears to end abruptly, Matthew narrates the promised rendezvous in Galilee, where the disciples worshipped Jesus (though some doubted). Then Jesus proclaims, 'All authority in heaven and on earth has been given to me' (Matt 28:18). He therefore commands them to make further disciples, to baptize them in the name of the Father, Son and Holy Spirit and to teach them to obey all that he has commanded. What is extraordinary about this is the way that Jesus now appears to be the mouthpiece for Christian doctrine. One might expect a command to baptize in his name, but here we have the trinitarian formula that was to become the mark of Christian orthodoxy. Could Jesus have said this? Conservatives will answer in the affirmative. If Jesus is the Son of God, who has been raised from the dead, of course he would not only know about the Trinity, but would be fully aware of his place within the Godhead. But it is not quite as simple as that, for if we look at the rest of the New Testament, we find that the early church baptized in the name of Jesus (Acts 2:38; 8:16; 10:48; 19:5; Rom 6:3), not in the name of Father, Son and Holy Spirit. Can we accept that a few weeks after Jesus gave this command, they forgot it until it was revived in the second century? Most scholars prefer the view that Matthew has simply inserted the formula that was being used in his church (e.g. Gundry, 1994, p. 596), just as he inserted his version of the Lord's Prayer (compare Matthew 6:9–13 with Luke 11:2–4).

The Gospel ends with the promise, 'I am with you always, to the end of the age' (28:20), mirroring the beginning of the Gospel, where *Emmanuel* was explained as 'God with us' (1:23). Furthermore, the church is given the promise that when 'two or three are gathered in my name, I am there among them' (18:20). Thus a significant aspect of Matthew's Christology is the presence of God in the story of Jesus, a story that did not come to an end with the crucifixion (Luz, 1995, p. 32). As we will see later, Matthew does not go so far as John, who speaks of a pre-existent relationship between God and Jesus. But he does speak of the presence of God in Jesus and the ongoing presence of Jesus in the Christian community.

Differences from Mark

It is very difficult to posit a consistent rationale for all of Matthew's differences from Mark. Most scholars believe them to be deliberate changes by Matthew, though other explanations are possible. For example, it may be that he had more than one version of a story and sometimes chose that rather than Mark's. Or he may have used an earlier version of Mark, which was later revised (Luz, 1995, p. 7). Some of the differences which are thought to be significant are the following:

The voice crying out in the wilderness (Matthew 3:3)
Mark opens his Gospel with a quotation from 'the prophet Isaiah' (1:2). But what immediately follows are words from Malachi 3:1 and Exodus 23:20 ('See, I am sending my messenger ahead of you, who will prepare your way'). Only after that do we find the words of Isaiah 40:3 ('Prepare the way of the Lord, make his paths straight'). Most scholars believe that Matthew has 'corrected' Mark, moving the Malachi/Exodus quotation to later in the Gospel (11:10) so that words from Isaiah follow the ascription. Those who transmitted the Gospel manuscripts took a different course; they changed Mark's 'the prophet Isaiah' to the plural 'the prophets' (the reading found in the King James Bible).

Plucking corn on the Sabbath (Matthew 12:1–8)
Mark's stark account seems to suggest that 'one such as I' (or 'Son of Man') is free to break the law (Mark 2:23–8). Matthew agrees with most of Mark's wording but has a quotation of Hosea 6:6 ('I desire mercy and not sacrifice'), which offers something of an explanation. This Old Testament text is clearly of some importance to Matthew as he also includes it in his story of the calling of Levi/Matthew (9:13).

Parable purpose (Matthew 13:10–15)
In using the Greek word *hina*, Mark appears to say that Jesus told parables 'in order that' those who are outside might be kept from seeing (Mark 4:12). Matthew also has this saying but uses the Greek word *hoste*, implying that this was the *result* of speaking in parables but not necessarily their *purpose*.

Miracles in his home town (Matthew 13:54–8)
Mark bluntly tells us that Jesus 'could do no deed of power there, except that he laid his hands on a few sick people and cured them' (Mark 6:5). Matthew appears to 'explain' this by saying that Jesus did not do many miracles there 'because of their unbelief'.

The conclusion to the 'walking on water' incident (Matthew 14:32–3)
At the end of this incident, Mark condemns the disciples 'for they did not understand about the loaves, but their hearts were hardened' (Mark 6:52). Matthew concludes on a much more positive note ('And those in the boat worshipped him, saying, "Truly you are the Son of God"'). Mark never has the disciples calling Jesus 'Son of God'.

Peter's confession (Matthew 16:16–19)
In Mark, there is some ambiguity as to how Jesus regarded Peter's confession (Mark 8:29–30). In Matthew, not only does Peter's confession include the words 'the Son of the living God' (cf. last example), but Jesus congratulates him and gives him this special promise:

> Blessed are you, Simon son of Jonah! For flesh and blood has not revealed this to you, but my Father in heaven. And I tell you, you are Peter, and on this rock I will build my church, and the gates of Hades will not prevail against it. I will give you the keys of the kingdom of heaven, and whatever you bind on earth will be bound in heaven, and whatever you loose on earth will be loosed in heaven.

Matthew's portrait of Jesus

Founder of the church

Matthew's Gospel is the only Gospel to use the Greek word *ekklesia*. The choice of the twelve disciples to parallel the twelve tribes of Israel was clearly an act of community formation, though this is never made explicit in Mark (contrast Matthew 19:28). But in the Greek of Matthew's Gospel, Jesus is reported as saying, 'I will build my church' (16:18). And in chapter 18, specific instructions are given to 'tell it to the church' (18:17). This emphasis on 'the church' can also be seen in the parable of the lost sheep. In Luke, the conclusion to the parable is that 'there will be more joy in heaven over one sinner who repents than over ninety-nine righteous people who need no repentance' (Luke 15:7). But in Matthew, it is about members of the church who go astray (Matt 18:10–14). John Riches explains:

> Whereas Luke refers to the 'lost' sheep (Lk. 15.4) and explains the parable in terms of repentance (v. 7), Matthew speaks about the sheep 'going astray' (Mt. 18.12) and explains the parable in terms of 'not being lost' (v. 14). Luke's parable is about bringing those outside the group in; Matthew's about the need to do all in one's power to ensure that the erring member is not finally lost to the group. Matthew's concern here is clearly that of the pastor who is seeking all

means in his power to hold his congregation together (1996, p. 74).

The careful arrangement of the teaching into five blocks facilitates Matthew's use as an instruction manual for church leaders: they deal with conduct, mission, the kingdom, settling disputes and waiting for the end. In Mark, discipleship means 'take up your cross', that is, be willing to die for Christ. Matthew agrees with this but also offers practical advice on living in community, embarking on mission and waiting for the arrival of God's kingdom. Thus according to Powell, one of the reasons for writing Matthew's Gospel was probably that the author felt that 'Mark contains no effective doctrine of the church' (1998, p. 75).

Son of God

For Jack Kingsbury (1988), 'Son of God' is the key title in Matthew, the one that interprets and gives content to all the others. Thus in Peter's confession, Jesus is not just Messiah but 'Son of the living God' (16:16). The high priest not only asks if Jesus is the Messiah but whether he is the 'Son of God' (26:63). The disciples worship him as 'Son of God' in the conclusion of the 'walking on water' incident (14:33). The crowd at the crucifixion criticize Jesus because he called himself 'Son of God' (27:43). The infancy stories stress that Jesus is God's Son. The three specific temptations revolve around sonship ('If you are the Son of God...'). And most significant of all, Jesus declares:

> All things have been handed over to me by my Father; and no one knows the Son except the Father, and no one knows the Father except the Son and anyone to whom the Son chooses to reveal him. (11:27)

In Mark, Jesus only speaks obliquely of himself as 'Son' (12:6; 13:32), but in Matthew there is an explicit reference to an intimate relationship between Father and Son. Schnackenburg says of this verse that the 'mutual knowledge of Father and Son is a loving familiarity, a knowledge that approaches a vision of each other's essence' (1995, p. 98). This is perhaps reading too much into a single verse, though as we will see in Chapter 5, it would be an accurate description of John's Gospel. But it does mark an 'advance' (in the sense of being more explicit) on what is said in Mark's Gospel.

King of Israel

However, alongside these 'Christian' categories must be set the fact that Matthew is commonly recognized as the most Jewish of the Gospels (cf. the early testimony that it was composed in Hebrew). Whether or not Bacon is correct in seeing the five discourses as a parallel to the Torah, the allusions to Israel's history are certainly extensive. Jesus is described as the 'son of David' (nine times). In contrast to the hateful King Herod, Jesus is Israel's true king. He has come to fulfil the law, not abrogate it (5:17). Indeed, contrary to popular belief, his ministry was not to everyone but to the 'lost sheep of the house of Israel' (10:6; 15:24). He assumes that the disciples will continue in traditional Jewish piety ('When you fast...') and even advises obedience to what the Pharisees teach (23:3), though not to what they do.

Thus we should not be too hasty in assuming that Matthew presents Jesus as the model of ecclesiastical orthodoxy. The title 'Son of God' might be bursting the wineskins of traditional Jewish interpretation(s) but it is still some way from the later Christian creeds. And though Jesus appears as 'founder of the church', it should be remembered that he was a Jew, not a Christian. His concern in his earthly life was a mission to fellow Jews, even prohibiting his disciples from preaching to outsiders. And when he wants an illustration of an outcast, the person who will not listen to the church is to be regarded as a 'Gentile and a tax-collector' (18:17). For some, this is evidence that the author of the Gospel is unlikely to be either a Gentile or a tax-collector.

Critic of Judaism

Not only is Matthew the most Jewish of the four Gospels, it also contains the most extreme critique of Judaism. Two passages stand out in particular. In the trial, the Jews are made to say: 'His blood be on us and on our children!' (27:25). Whatever Matthew's intention in writing this (it did not come from Mark), it has fuelled the most horrific anti-Semitism down the centuries. And if we are tempted to write this off as simply Matthew's bigotry (as some do), chapter 23 has Jesus delivering a terrible series of woes against the Pharisees. It has often led to a caricature of first-century Judaism as 'petty-fogging legalism'. But Sanders (1985, 1993) has challenged this picture. There are no extant texts, he says, which suggest that first-century Jews believed they had to earn their salvation. Far from it; despite the diversity and forms of Judaism in the first century, they were united in their view that they were inheritors of a covenant of grace. And when they did sin, the sacrificial system was there to restore the relationship.

Most commentators believe that Matthew has allowed his own experience of conflict between church and synagogue to influence his portrait of Jesus here. Schnackenburg, for example, says that Matthew 23 'bears the special signature of the evangelist, who fills it with his criticism of contemporary Judaism' (1995, p. 83). And Matthew's frequent references to *their* synagogues and *their* teachers (4:23; 7:29; 9:35; 10:17; 13:54) tends to support this. On the other hand, others have pointed out that Jesus' criticisms are no worse than that of an Amos or Jeremiah, so that the epithet of 'anti-Semitist' is misguided. Jesus did have some strong things to say to his contemporaries but that does not amount to anti-Semitism. It is a critique from within, not racism from without.

Conclusion

By incorporating almost all of Mark into his Gospel, Matthew naturally shares many of its characteristics. But he has developed the picture of Jesus to bring out his own particular emphases. Jesus is the founder of the church. He is Son of God, a figure worthy of worship, whose presence with the disciples fulfils the promise of *Emmanuel*, God with us. He is Israel's true king, the promised Messiah, whose earthly ministry was confined to the Jewish people. But the scope is ultimately universal. Jesus' command is to go and make disciples from all the nations. And as churches sprang up throughout the known world, they adopted Matthew's Gospel as the 'church Gospel'. It told them of their foundations, transmitted Jesus' teaching in topical blocks, and pointed them towards the coming of the kingdom. From the evidence of later centuries, Matthew's Gospel must go down as one of the most successful revisions ever made. On the other hand, some would argue that it began the process whereby Mark was 'toned down', a process that is even more apparent in Luke's attempt to provide Theophilus with an 'orderly account'.

4

Luke's Gospel

Like Matthew, Luke differs from Mark by including infancy stories, resurrection appearances and additional teaching. However, the infancy stories and resurrection appearances are completely different from those in Matthew and the teaching is not interspersed in blocks. Most of the teaching falls within an extended travel narrative (Luke 9:51 – 18:14), which comes between the healing of the epileptic boy (Mark 9) and the rich young ruler (Mark 10). It is here that we find Luke's most famous parables, such as the good Samaritan (Luke 10), great banquet (Luke 14), prodigal son (Luke 15), shrewd manager (Luke 16), Lazarus and Dives (Luke 16), and the persistent widow (Luke 18). By placing them all here, Luke manages to insert a great deal of teaching material without disrupting the basic order of Mark.

Some of this extra teaching finds parallels in Matthew's five blocks. For example, from the sermon on the mount (Matt 6:9–13), Luke has a version of the Lord's Prayer (Luke 11:2–4). From the Mission discourse (Matt 10:34–6), he has the sayings about Jesus causing division in families (Luke 12:49–53). From the kingdom chapter (Matt 13:33), he has the yeast parable (Luke 13:21). From the church discourse (Matt 18:12–14), he has the parable of the lost sheep (Luke 15:4–7). And from the apocalyptic discourse (Matt 24:37–8), he has the comparison of the end-times with the days of Noah (Luke 17:26–7).

Michael Goulder (1989) believes that Luke has taken this material from Matthew but most scholars think it is more likely that Matthew and Luke both drew on a sayings source, commonly called Q (from the German *Quelle*, meaning 'source'). Matthew used it to form his five discourses, perhaps on the model of the Pentateuch. Luke used it to construct his travel narrative. If this is correct, it would explain why the wording of the sayings is often very similar, though the context in which they appear is frequently different. It also means that Mark may not be our earliest source for the life of Jesus, since many scholars (who accept Q) believe that it pre-dates Mark. This has been particularly important to members of the Jesus Seminar, as we shall see later (in Chapters 6 and 8).

Infancy stories (chapters 1–2)

If Matthew's account focuses on Joseph and Bethlehem, Luke's account focuses on Mary and Jerusalem. The impression given by Matthew is that Joseph lived in Bethlehem (Matt 1:18–2:2), fled to Egypt to avoid the wrath of Herod (2:14) and only 'made his home in a town called Nazareth' (2:23) after Herod had died. The action is controlled by the angelic messages to Joseph, first to make him aware of the extraordinary pregnancy (1:20–1); then to tell him to flee to Egypt (2:13); thirdly to tell him to return to Israel (2:19–20); and lastly, to tell him to settle in Nazareth (2:22).

In Luke, we are told that Mary was already living in Nazareth when an angel visited and told *her* about the pregnancy (Luke 1:26–38). She then visited her relative Elizabeth, who was also pregnant, and stayed for three months. Then, because of the census (not mentioned by Matthew), Joseph and Mary made their way to Bethlehem, where she gave birth to Jesus 'and laid him in a manger, because there was no place for them in the inn' (2:7). Eight days later, they took Jesus to be circumcised (2:21) and when the time of purification was completed (40 days), they went to the temple to offer the designated sacrifices ('a pair of turtle-doves or two young pigeons').

After these religious observances were completed, they returned to Nazareth where Jesus 'grew and became strong' (2:40: no flight to Egypt is mentioned). Each year they returned to Jerusalem for the Passover festival and on one such occasion, when Jesus was 12 years old, his parents began the journey home without him. When they returned to look for him they found him discussing and debating with the teachers of the law (2:46). Though very restrained compared with later infancy narratives (see Chapter 6), there is something of the 'child prodigy' motif present in Luke.

Luke also includes a genealogy of Jesus but he places it at the end of chapter 3, rather than beginning his Gospel with it. It contains a number of interesting features. For example, it begins by telling us that 'Jesus was about thirty years old when he began his work', our only reference to Jesus' age (though see John 8:57). When he says that Jesus was the 'son of Joseph', he is mindful of the virgin birth and adds 'as was thought' (Luke 3:23). And whereas Matthew's genealogy goes back to Abraham, the father of Israel, Luke takes it back to Adam, the father of the human race. Most commentators think this is because Luke is a Gentile writing to Gentiles, though whether he is the physician mentioned elsewhere in the New Testament (Col 4:14; 2 Tim 4:11; Phil 24) is disputed (see Appendix).

Furthermore, apart from the line from Abraham to David and the mention of Zerubbabel, Luke has a completely different set of names to Matthew (and a great many more), including a different father for Joseph. One suggestion for the latter is that Matthew has given us the line through Joseph, whereas Luke traces it through Mary (Heli becomes Mary's father, who adopted Joseph as heir because Mary was an only child). However, there is also a different set of names from David to Zerubbabel, so that Nolland (1989, p. 174) suggests we should probably look for theological rather than historical explanations for these discrepancies. He sees this in the taking of the genealogy back to Adam (who is 'Son of God') and through Nathan rather than Solomon, because Solomon's line is said to have come to an end in Jeremiah 22:24–30.

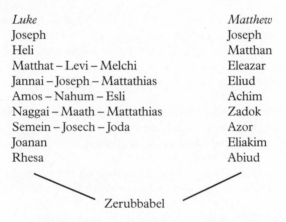

Luke	*Matthew*
Joseph	Joseph
Heli	Matthan
Matthat – Levi – Melchi	Eleazar
Jannai – Joseph – Mattathias	Eliud
Amos – Nahum – Esli	Achim
Naggai – Maath – Mattathias	Zadok
Semein – Josech – Joda	Azor
Joanan	Eliakim
Rhesa	Abiud

Zerubbabel

Resurrection appearances (chapter 24)

The promise of a reunion between Jesus and the disciples in Galilee (Mark 16:7) is fulfilled in Matthew. Luke, however, records only appearances in Jerusalem and this appears to be deliberate, for the angel's words at the tomb have been recast:

Mark 16:6–7	*Luke 24:5–7*
Do not be alarmed; you are looking for Jesus of Nazareth, who was crucified. He has been raised; he is not here. Look, there is the place they laid him. But go, tell his disciples and Peter *that he is going ahead of you to Galilee*; there	Why do you look for the living among the dead? He is not here, but has risen. Remember how he told you, *while he was still in Galilee*, that the Son of Man

| you will see him, just as he told you. | must be handed over to sinners, and be crucified, and on the third day rise again. |

Several features stand out in Luke's resurrection stories. First, the bodily nature of the resurrection is emphasized. The disciples are invited to touch Jesus' hands and feet and he eats a meal in front of them (Luke 24:39–43). Secondly, Jesus explains how the scriptures speak about him (24:45–7). Unfortunately, we are not given any specific passages or interpretations; only that 'everything written about me in the law of Moses, the prophets, and the psalms must be fulfilled'. Thirdly, given that Luke has also written a sequel to the Gospel ('The Acts of the Apostles'), where the disciples meet to break bread and pray (Acts 2:46), the fact that Cleopas and his friend recognized Jesus when he broke the bread (Luke 24:30–1) takes on special significance. As Talbert says, the story 'not only serves as a bridge between the meals the earthly Jesus had with his disciples and the later church's Eucharist, it also says that at such meals the presence of the risen Lord was known: Jesus is alive and one place of his recognition is at the breaking of bread' (1982, p. 230). Talbert also offers this insightful comment:

> The distinctiveness of this understanding of the Eucharist may be seen when it is compared with that of the fourth Gospel and of Paul. In the fourth Gospel the Eucharist is the cultic extension of the incarnation: through its physical elements one experiences contact with the divine world just as one did through the flesh of Jesus in the days of his incarnation (cf. John 6). In Paul the Lord's Supper is the moment in which one remembers (identifies with, participates in) Jesus' death much as the Israelites-Jews remembered (participated in) the events of the Exodus at their Passover meal (cf. 1 Corinthians 11). Luke sees the Supper as the extension of the meals with the earthly Jesus and in anticipation of the messianic banquet, a meal at which one experiences the presence of Christ as the disciples did after the resurrection (1982, p. 231).

Lastly, Luke ends his Gospel with a description of the ascension, where Jesus 'led them out as far as Bethany, and, lifting up his hands, he blessed them. While he was blessing them, he withdrew from them and was carried up into heaven' (Luke 24:50–1). This is slightly puzzling since all the events of Luke 24 appear to take place on the same day (vv. 13,36,50), suggesting that Jesus ascended on the evening of Easter Sunday. But Acts 1:1–8 states that Jesus was with them for 40 days before the ascension. Since the same author wrote both works (Acts 1:1), one can only presume that Luke is saving the 40 days for the sequel and so passes straight to the ascension in Luke 24:50–2.

Travel narrative (9:51 – 18:14)

Opinions vary as to whether this section should be called a 'travel narrative'. The very stylized beginning ('When the days drew near for him to be taken up, he set his face to go to Jerusalem') marks it out as special and we are given reminders of the journey at Luke 13:22 and 17:11. But Luke's interest is hardly geographical. Jesus is on his way to Jerusalem 'because it is impossible for a prophet to be killed away from Jerusalem' (13:33). He has an appointment with 'what must be' (9:22; 17:25; 22:37; 24:7). Evans (1990, pp. 34–6) thinks the inspiration for presenting teaching within the framework of a journey comes from the book of Deuteronomy. He notes that the journey begins with Jesus sending disciples to go ahead of him, as did Moses (Luke 10:1–16; Deut 1). He gives them the double commandment to love God and neighbour, just as Moses gave the ten commandments (Luke 10:25–7; Deut 5). He tells them how he has bound the stronger one, just as Moses gave instructions about defeating stronger nations (Luke 11:14–26; Deut 9–10). He speaks about clean and unclean (Luke 11:37 – 12:12; Deut 12) and communal judgement (Luke 12:54 – 13:5; Deut 13). And the discussion of inheritance rights for good and bad sons (Deut 21) forms an interesting background to the parable of the prodigal son (Luke 15:11–32). Not all of Evans' parallels are convincing but it remains an interesting hypothesis.

Like Matthew, Luke has a set of 'woes' against the Pharisees, though the settings in each are very different. In Matthew, the woes follow disputes about 'paying taxes to Caesar' and 'marriage at the resurrection' (Matt 23). In Luke, they occur much earlier in the narrative, while Jesus is dining with a Pharisee (Luke 11:37–53). Astounded that Jesus did not wash his hands before eating (a dispute about ritual, not hygiene), the Pharisees are denounced by Jesus for:

1. cleaning the outside of cups but being full of greed and wickedness
2. tithing herbs but neglecting justice and love
3. wanting the seats of honour
4. being like unmarked graves
5. loading people with burdens and doing nothing to help
6. building the tombs of the prophets whom their ancestors killed
7. being guilty of the blood shed from Abel to Zechariah
8. taking away the key of knowledge.

All of these are present in Matthew 23 but in the order 5, 3, 8, 2, 1, 4, 6, 7. If these come from Q, as many scholars believe, then this sayings source had some very strong things to say about contemporary

Judaism. Prophets have been sent to warn Israel but they have been killed or abused. As a result, this generation is guilty of

> the blood of all the prophets shed since the foundation of the world, from the blood of Abel to the blood of Zechariah, who perished between the altar and the sanctuary. Yes, I tell you, it will be charged against this generation. (Luke 11:49–51 = Matt 23:35–6)

Luke's travel narrative is also the setting for the Lord's Prayer. In Matthew, this occurs in the sermon on the mount, along with the beatitudes. But in Luke, the beatitudes occur in 6:20–3, while the Lord's Prayer comes in 11:2–4. The form of the prayer is also different. It is of course possible that Jesus said this prayer on many occasions and Matthew and Luke have reported two of them. But the solemn nature of it ('When you pray, say') suggests that it was special and intended to be memorized. Most scholars believe that when Matthew and Luke reached the place where they wished to incorporate the prayer, they cited it in the form that was being used in their respective churches.

Luke's omissions from Mark

Since Luke uses only about 30 per cent of Mark, one must be cautious about explaining why Luke has omitted a particular story or saying. For example, Luke omits the story of the Syrophoenician woman (Mark 7:24–30) and it could be argued that this is because he was not comfortable with Jesus calling her a dog. But actually, this is simply part of a larger omission, for Luke omits all the material between Mark's two feeding stories (Mark 6:45 – 8:26), perhaps because he thought it was repetitious, perhaps because the version of Mark he was using was defective. Nevertheless, there are some omissions which, when taken together, seem to point to the themes of 'greater reverence' and 'avoiding offence'.

For example, in the story of the man with the withered hand (Luke 6:6–11), he omits Mark's reference to Jesus' anger (Mark 3:5). In the preface to the Beelzebul story (Luke 11:14–23), he omits Mark's comment that Jesus' family sought to restrain him (Mark 3:21). Peter does not rebuke Jesus after his confession (Luke 9:18–22) and hence does not receive the 'Get behind me, Satan' rebuke (Mark 8:33). When the disciples try to prevent people bringing children to Jesus (Luke 18:15–17), Luke does not mention Jesus' indignation (Mark 10:14). In the apocalyptic discourse (Luke 21:5–33), he leaves out the saying that even the Son does not know when the 'hour' will come (Mark 13:32); and Mark's slightly worrying saying, 'the one who endures to the end will be saved' (Mark 13:13) is phrased more positively, 'By your endurance you will gain your souls' (Luke 21:19). In Gethsemane, Luke omits Jesus' words, 'I am deeply grieved, even to death' (Mark 14:34), and says the disciples fell asleep only once 'because of grief' (Luke 22:45). He omits the cry of dereliction on the cross (Mark 15:34) and, far from having the women leaving the empty tomb saying 'nothing to anyone, for they were afraid' (Mark 16:8), Luke says, 'returning from the tomb, they told all this to the eleven and to all the rest' (Luke 24:9).

A particular omission that has caused much discussion is Mark's 'ransom' saying. In a discussion over who is to be regarded as the greatest, Jesus replies that among the Gentiles, rulers lord it over their subjects – but that is not how it is to be among them (Mark 10:35–43; Luke 22:24–6). Jesus then says:

> ... but whoever wishes to become great among you must be your servant, and whoever wishes to be first among you must be slave of all. For the Son of Man came not to be served but to serve, *and to give his life a ransom for many.* (Mark 10:45)

> ... rather the greatest among you must become like the youngest, and the leader like one who serves. For who is greater, the one who is at the table or the one who serves? Is it not the one at the table? But I am among you as one who serves. (Luke 22:26–7)

Talbert thinks that Luke is deliberately avoiding the idea that Jesus died as a sacrifice for sins. Rather, 'Luke portrays the death of Jesus as a martyrdom, the unjust murder of an innocent man by the established powers due to the pressure of the Jewish leaders' (1982, p. 212). As well as the omission of Mark's ransom saying, Talbert notes three other points. First, in the evangelistic speeches in Acts, both Peter (2:38; 3:19; 5:31; 10:43) and Paul (13:38; 17:30; 26:18) preach the forgiveness of sins but never in connection with Jesus' death. Secondly, Luke twice quotes from Isaiah 53 (Luke 22:37; Acts 8:32–3) but on neither occasion does the quotation come from the 'vicarious' part of the chapter. Thirdly, in Luke–Acts, neither baptism (Acts 2:38; 8:12; 9:18; 10:47; 16:15; 19:5; 22:16) nor the Lord's supper (Luke 22:16–20; 24:30; Acts 2:42–6; 20:7; 27:35) are connected with Jesus' atoning death. This is a formidable case, though it should be noted that Talbert's reading of the last supper narrative (Luke 22:16–20) is open to question and Luke frequently stresses the (divine) necessity of Jesus' death (Luke 9:22; 13:33; 17:25; 24:7).

Luke's changes to Mark

According to J.M. Creed, 'An examination of Luke's treatment of the Marcan text shews him to have carried through a drastic revision of the language. The characteristic Marcan idioms are obliterated, and the whole narrative is made smoother and more consecutive' (1957, p. lxi). Though one must be careful of value judgements, Luke appears more sophisticated than Mark, improving his grammar and ironing out many of his ambiguities. Thus instead of the 'forsaken' saying on the cross, Luke has three sayings, all of which are positive. The first is the forgiveness saying, 'Father, forgive them; for they do not know what they are doing' (23:34). The second is the promise to the penitent thief that 'today you will be with me in Paradise' (23:43). It should be noted that as well as a promise to the thief, it is also an expression of his own confidence; today he will be in paradise. The third, Jesus' final saying from the cross, is the much more reverent sounding, 'Father, into your hands I commend my spirit' (23:46). If Talbert is correct in thinking that Luke presents Jesus as an example of martyrdom, then this is what Christians should emulate, not a demand to know why God has forsaken them.

Mark begins his account of Jesus' public ministry by saying that Jesus proclaimed, 'The time is fulfilled, and the kingdom of God has come near' (Mark 1:15). Luke appears to have rephrased this so as to omit the note of urgency ('Then Jesus, filled with the power of the Spirit, returned to Galilee, and a report about him spread through all the surrounding country', Luke 4:14). Furthermore, when Mark has Jesus say that there are 'some standing here who will not taste death until they see that the kingdom of God has come with power' (Mark 9:1), Luke makes its meaning less specific by omitting the final phrase 'has come with power' (Luke 9:27). In other words, they might see the kingdom coming but not necessarily 'in power'. What is perplexing and perhaps disturbing in Mark is alleviated (though not eliminated) in Luke.

One further change is worth mentioning. In Mark, the 'rejection at Nazareth' story comes between the raising of Jairus' daughter (5:35–43) and the mission of the twelve (Mark 6:7–13). In Luke, the sending out of the twelve immediately follows the raising of Jairus' daughter (Luke 8:49 – 9:6), with the 'rejection at Nazareth' story transferred to the very beginning of Jesus' public ministry (Luke 4:16–30) and given a specific setting: Jesus reads from Isaiah 61 and declares that, 'Today this scripture has been fulfilled in your hearing' (4:21). The effect is to make the liberation themes of Isaiah 61 programmatic for understanding Jesus' ministry. Jesus is God's anointed prophet who has come to 'bring good news to the poor... to proclaim release to the captives and recovery of sight to the blind, to let the oppressed go free, to proclaim the year of the Lord's favour' (4:18–19).

Luke's portrait of Jesus

Prophet

As we have just noted, Luke begins Jesus' public ministry with the Nazareth sermon, where Jesus declares, 'The Spirit of the Lord is upon me' (Luke 4:18). In the story of the raising of the widow's son at Nain (which parallels Elijah's miracle in 1 Kings 17:17–24), the crowd conclude, 'A great prophet has risen among us!' (Luke 7:16). During the travel narrative, Jesus must reach his goal 'because it is impossible for a prophet to be killed away from Jerusalem' (13:33). And on the road to Emmaus, the disconsolate disciples speak of Jesus as a 'prophet mighty in deed and word before God and all the people' (24:19). Whatever else he might be, Luke clearly portrays Jesus as a great prophet (Wright, 1996, pp. 145–97).

Friend of outcasts and sinners

Richard Burridge (1994) uses the ancient symbol of the ox/calf as 'bearer of burdens' to characterize Luke's presentation of Jesus. It is a humanitarian portrait, particularly concerned for the foreigner and outcast. Samaritans were regarded with particular disdain by the Jews but Jesus tells a parable which highlights the compassion of a Samaritan (Luke 10:25–37). When ten leprosy sufferers are healed, only one returns to show his gratitude, and it is a Samaritan (17:16). And when James and John want to call down fire on a Samaritan village, Jesus rebukes them (9:51–6).

Women figure prominently in Luke's Gospel. The infancy stories focus on Mary's role, rather than Joseph's. Indeed, Mary's response to the angel (1:38) is in direct contrast to that of Zechariah (1:18). We hear of Elizabeth, mother of John the Baptist (1:24), and Anna, who is called a prophet (2:36). We hear of Mary and Martha (10:38), the widow at Nain (7:12) and the woman who has been crippled for eighteen years (13:11). Women appear as Jesus' travelling companions and benefactors (8:1–3). And after the crucifixion, it is the women who discover the empty tomb. As Joel Green says, 'their faithful witness is set in contrast to the response of the male disciples, who regard their news as only idle talk (24:11) until it is confirmed by other men' (1995, p. 93).

This theme is exemplified in the crucifixion narrative. Mark's story is of almost unremitting darkness. In Luke, on the way to the cross, Jesus says to the daughters of Jerusalem, 'do not weep for me, but weep for yourselves and for your children' (23:28). And on the cross, he asks for his enemies' forgiveness (23:34 – though some manuscripts omit this verse) and offers words of comfort to the penitent thief (23:43).

Saviour of the world

Though Luke is clear that Jesus did not significantly engage with Gentiles in his earthly ministry, the universal aspect is stressed in a number of ways. We have already mentioned the extension of the genealogy to Adam. He also extends Mark's quotation of Isaiah 40:3 to include the words 'and all flesh shall see the salvation of God' (Luke 3:6). In the Nazareth rejection story, it is his mention of Elijah and Elisha ministering outside Israel which angers the people (4:28). Blame for Jesus' crucifixion is shifted towards the Jews with Pilate declaring three times that Jesus is innocent (23:4,14,22). Indeed, some have argued that the joint project of writing Luke–Acts was to show that Christianity is a religion worthy of the Roman empire, with both Jesus and Paul innocent of all charges. Certainly a number of things that might have caused offence have been removed.

According to Hans Conzelmann (1960), one of these 'offences' is that Mark appears to portray Jesus as predicting the imminent end of the world (Mark 1:15; 9:1; 13:30). Either because this was subversive or simply because it had not happened, Conzelmann argued that Luke wished to remove this emphasis and replace it with an indefinite church age. As well as the points already noted, there are two more that deserve mention. In his introduction to the parable of the pounds (Luke 19:11–27 = Matt 25:14–30), Luke says that Jesus told this parable 'because they supposed that the kingdom of God was to appear immediately' (19:11). And in the apocalyptic discourse, though Luke reproduces Mark's 'generation' saying, he inserts into the discourse the words, 'and Jerusalem will be trampled on by the Gentiles, until the times of the Gentiles are fulfilled' (21:24). Conzelmann argued from this that Luke divides history into three periods. The first is the time of preparation, the Old Testament period up to and including John the Baptist (16:16). The second is the earthly ministry of Jesus, the theme of Luke's first volume. This is why the original title of Conzelmann's book was *Die Mitte der Zeit* ('The middle of time'). The third period is the age of the church, 'the times of the Gentiles' and the theme of Luke's second volume.

This theory has been extremely influential and many scholars now speak of Luke writing a 'salvation history' (e.g. Tuckett, 1996, p. 34).

But there are problems. For example, if Luke is so concerned to remove Mark's imminent end, why does he retain the 'generation' saying (Mark 13:30 = Luke 21:32) and introduce parables about staying alert (thief in the night; servants awaiting their master's return)? Tom Wright (1996) has a rather different answer. He does not think that Mark presents Jesus as predicting the end of the world. Rather, language like 'the sun will be darkened, and the moon will not give its light' (Mark 13:24) is apocalyptic language referring to a great national crisis. It is not speaking about a 'cosmic meltdown' but using 'cosmic' language to warn of an impending judgement (as in Isaiah 34). If this is correct, then Luke may be heading off certain misunderstandings of Mark but is not fundamentally changing Jesus' message.

Lord

According to Acts, Peter concludes his Pentecost speech by saying, 'Therefore let the entire house of Israel know with certainty that God has made him both Lord and Messiah, this Jesus whom you crucified' (Acts 2:36). Luke is so convinced that 'Jesus is Lord' that he uses it almost unconsciously. For example, in Luke 12:42 he writes, 'And the Lord said'. In Luke 19:8, 'Zacchaeus stood there and said to the Lord'. But what did Luke understand by the term? Was it simply a statement of Luke's allegiance (like Rabbi or Master)? Or was it more than that? Some have argued that since the Greek translators of the Hebrew scriptures rendered the divine name (YHWH) by *Kyrios*, calling Jesus *Kyrios* is tantamount to calling him God. But we should note two things. First, it is unnecessary to suppose that all of the occurrences of *Kyrios* in Luke–Acts have the same meaning. It is clear that sometimes it is no more than the polite 'Sir' (Luke 7:6). Second, in those cases where an exalted meaning is intended (Luke 1:43 has Elizabeth calling Mary the 'mother of my Lord'), there is a conceptual difficulty that would take centuries to sort out. Put simply, how could Elizabeth possibly think that Mary's unborn child is the God she has worshipped all her life? It is a problem that comes to the fore even more in John's Gospel, as we shall see.

Conclusion

Luke is the longest of the four Gospels, both in the number of words and its scope (annunciations and births at one end, appearances and ascension at the other). It appears to have toned down some of the harshness and ambiguity of Mark, though it has taken from Q (or Matthew) stern judgements against the Pharisees. The long travel narrative contains some eight or nine chapters of teaching, which might give credence to the view that Jesus was an itinerant wisdom teacher. But as a whole, Luke presents Jesus as God's anointed, an Israelite prophet with a message of judgement for oppressors and compassion for the downtrodden. It is what many people imagine a biography of Jesus should be like – and what many people imagine Christians should be like. If Matthew produced a Gospel for the church, Luke produced a Gospel for the world.

5

John's Gospel

Despite the differences between Matthew, Mark and Luke, they are called the synoptic Gospels because they can be arranged in a synopsis (i.e. 'seen together'). They all follow the same basic story line. For example, despite minor variations in order, we can easily list twenty incidents that are common to all three:

1. Baptism by John
2. Temptation in the wilderness
3. Calling of disciples
4. Healing of Peter's mother-in-law
5. Healing of a paralytic
6. Calling of Levi/Matthew
7. Plucking corn on the Sabbath
8. Man with the withered hand
9. Parable of the sower
10. Stilling of the storm
11. Mission of the twelve
12. Feeding of the 5000
13. Peter's confession
14. Transfiguration
15. Rich young ruler
16. Blessing of the children
17. Triumphal entry on a donkey
18. Cleansing of the temple
19. Apocalyptic discourse
20. Last supper

However, when we come to John, we are immediately aware that we are reading a very different sort of Gospel. Of the twenty items listed above, only five are found in John (3, 12, 17, 18, 20), often with significant differences. For example, the cleansing of the temple comes right at the beginning of the Gospel (2:12–25), not at its climax. The last supper does not mention any special words over the bread and wine but describes Jesus washing the disciples' feet. And while Peter and Andrew are among the first disciples called by Jesus, their calling takes place in Judea while John is baptizing (1:35–42), not in Galilee after John has been arrested (Mark 1:14–20).

The feeding of the 5000 offers an important point of contact (John 6 = Mark 6) but unlike the synoptics, this is not part of a Galilean ministry, which is then followed by a single journey to Jerusalem. In John's Gospel, Jesus is frequently in Jerusalem (2:13; 5:1; 7:10; 10:22–3). Indeed, it is only because John mentions these festivals that Jesus' pub-

lic ministry is reckoned to be about three years. From the point of view
of time references, it would be possible to fit all of the events in the synoptic Gospels into a single year.

John's Gospel easily divides into four sections. Chapter 1 consists of
an extended prologue, the ministry of John the Baptist and the gathering of disciples. Chapters 2–12 consist of miracles and teaching,
though unlike the synoptics, there are no parables or exorcisms.
Chapters 13–20 form the passion narrative and the Gospel finishes
with a sort of appendix (21), which most scholars believe was added
later (20:30–1 looks like the original ending). The Gospel ends with
this claim:

> This is the disciple who is testifying to these things and has written
> them, and we know that his testimony is true. But there are also many
> other things that Jesus did; if every one of them were written down, I
> suppose that the world itself could not contain the books that would
> be written. (21:24–5)

This has traditionally been taken as evidence that the author of the
Gospel is the 'disciple whom Jesus loved' (21:20), namely John, son of
Zebedee (see Appendix). But it would be odd for John to say of himself, 'we know that his testimony is true'. It is more likely that the
author(s) of the Gospel (the 'we' in the above passage) are claiming to
have used *traditions* that go back to John. Thus it would appear that the
names that became associated with the Gospels (Matthew, Mark, Luke
and John) point more towards the source of the traditions than actual
authorship. In this, they parallel the way that Moses became associated
with the Torah, Solomon with wisdom and David with psalmody,
though much of this material is clearly not written by them (e.g.
Proverbs 30–1; Psalms 73–85).

Introduction (chapter 1)

Though John begins with an introduction which includes a
Christological statement, narrative concerning John the Baptist and the
call of the first disciples, each of these is strikingly different from their
synoptic counterparts. For example, Mark's Christological statement
consists of a single verse ('The beginning of the good news of Jesus
Christ, the Son of God'). John has eighteen verses describing the person of Christ, his relationship to God and his role in salvation:

> In the beginning was the Word (*logos*), and the Word was with God,
> and the Word was God. He was in the beginning with God. All things
> came into being through him... in him was life, and the life was the
> light of all people... The true light, which enlightens everyone, was

coming into the world... He came to what was his own, and his own people did not accept him. But to all who received him, who believed in his name, he gave power to become children of God... And the Word became flesh and lived among us, and we have seen his glory, the glory as of a father's only son, full of grace and truth... From his fullness we have all received, grace upon grace... No one has ever seen God. It is God the only Son, who is close to the Father's heart, who has made him known. (John 1:1–18; abbreviated)

It is generally agreed that John is drawing on the idea of divine wisdom to describe Jesus as the agent of creation and redemption (see Proverbs 8). Paul calls Jesus the 'wisdom of God' (1 Cor 1:24) and the theme appears in other hymnic passages in the New Testament (Col 1:15–20; Heb 1:1–3). However, John focuses his thought around the idea of the divine *logos* 'which enlightens everyone'. This idea had a rich history in some strands of Greek thought (such as Stoicism), and some believe that John chose it in order to appeal to a Hellenistic audience. But the Dead Sea Scrolls have shown that such ideas are by no means alien to Hebrew thought. Indeed, since Judea had been subject to Hellenistic influence for nearly three centuries, the two backgrounds need not be seen as mutually exclusive.

Like the synoptics, John presents the Baptist as Jesus' forerunner and even includes in 1:23 the same quotation from Isaiah 40:3 ('I am the voice of one crying out in the wilderness, "Make straight the way of the Lord"'). But there are three notable differences in John's presentation. First, he is at pains to show that John is inferior to Jesus and claimed nothing for himself. Even in the glorious prologue, he inserts the comment that John 'was not the light' (1:8). When the narrative begins (1:19–28), John is asked a series of questions ('Who are you?'; 'Are you Elijah?'; 'Are you the prophet?'), each of which he denies ('I am not the Messiah'; 'I am not'; 'No'). And later in chapter 3, when 'a discussion about purification arose between John's disciples and a Jew' (3:25), John the Baptist says of Jesus, 'He must increase, but I must decrease' (3:30). Clearly there is to be no confusion as to who is the superior.

The second difference is that John the Baptist's testimony to Jesus is far more explicit. For example, when he sees Jesus, he says, 'Here is the Lamb of God who takes away the sin of the world' (1:29). And a few verses later, we read, 'I myself have seen and have testified that this is the Son of God' (1:34). Thus John the Baptist is presented as having explicit knowledge of both the person and work of Christ (cf. Luke 7:19).

The third difference is perhaps the most surprising of all, for John's

Gospel does not actually narrate the baptism of Jesus. Indeed, our author seems to have gone to great lengths to give us the details without narrating the event. Thus the Baptist testifies that Jesus is the one sent from God, for he saw 'the Spirit descending from heaven like a dove, and it remained on him' (1:32). But the actual baptism of Jesus is not narrated. Why? One suggestion is that disciples of the Baptist (Acts 18:25) were claiming that John must have been greater than Jesus for he not only came first but was the one who baptized Jesus. Another suggestion is that perhaps the author is making a polemical point about the sacraments, since John's Gospel also omits the institution of the Eucharist. We will say more about this later.

Finally, John and the synoptics narrate the calling of the first disciples but there the similarity ends. In the synoptics, they are fishing in the Sea of Galilee when Jesus passes by and says to them, 'Follow me and I will make you fish for people' (Mark 1:17). At once, they leave their nets and follow Jesus. In John, we learn that the disciples were formerly disciples of John the Baptist and that Andrew goes to fetch Simon with the words, 'We have found the Messiah' (1:41). When Simon comes to Jesus, he is given a change of name:

> The next day John again was standing with two of his disciples, and as he watched Jesus walk by, he exclaimed, 'Look, here is the Lamb of God!' The two disciples heard him say this, and they followed Jesus... One of the two who heard John speak and followed him was Andrew, Simon Peter's brother. He first found his brother Simon and said to him, 'We have found the Messiah' (which is translated Anointed). He brought Simon to Jesus, who looked at him and said, 'You are Simon son of John. You are to be called Cephas' (which is translated Peter).

The book of signs (chapters 2–12)

Unlike the numerous healings and exorcisms in the synoptic Gospels, John selects just seven stories, which he calls *semeia* ('signs'). The feeding of the 5000 and the walking on water are found in the synoptics but the other five are unique to John:

1. Water into wine (2:1–11)
2. Official's son (4:43–54)
3. Invalid at the pool (5:1–14)
4. Feeding of the 5000 (6:1–14)
5. Walking on water (6:16–21)
6. Blind man (9:1–12)
7. Raising of Lazarus (11:1–43)

It is interesting that there are no exorcisms in John, despite the fact that Jesus is accused of having a demon on three occasions (7:20; 8:48; 10:21). Also interesting is the way that the last five of these 'signs' all lead into a long discourse about who Jesus is and where he comes from. Indeed, in the case of the invalid at the pool, the healing (5:1–14) seems almost inconsequential compared with the discourse that follows (5:15–47). The story of the feeding of the 5000 leads to Jesus' acclamation, 'I am the bread of life. Whoever comes to me will never be hungry, and whoever believes in me will never be thirsty' (6:35). The raising of Lazarus gives Jesus the opportunity to proclaim, 'I am the resurrection and the life. Those who believe in me, even though they die, will live, and everyone who lives and believes in me will never die' (11:25–6). Indeed, it appears to be by design that there are seven such sayings:

1. I am the bread of life (6:35)
2. I am the light of the world (8:12)
3. I am the gate for the sheep (10:7)
4. I am the good shepherd (10:11)
5. I am the resurrection and the life (11:25)
6. I am the way, and the truth, and the life (14:6)
7. I am the true vine (15:1)

Each of these begins with the revelation formula *ego eimi*. This has a rich history in profane and sacred literature and most commentators refer to the discussion found in Rudolph Bultmann's famous commentary (1971, pp. 225–6). He says that the expression is used in four different ways. It is used to describe who someone is ('I am Ploutos'; 'I am El-Shaddai') or what they are ('I am a shepherd'; 'I am the first and the last'). Then it can be used to identify the subject with a given action ('I am he who arose as Chepre'; 'I am the one who brought you out of Egypt') or as a recognition formula ('I am the one you are looking for'). A particularly important background is the Greek translation (LXX) of Exodus 3:14, where the Hebrew is rendered *ego eimi ho on* (literally, 'I am the one who is'). John's use of these seven *ego eimi* sayings, along with the seven signs and many discourses, led Bultmann to describe this section of the Gospel as 'The Revelation of the Glory to the World'.

The passion narrative (chapters 13–20)

The second half of the Gospel is the passion story but again with some surprising differences. First, while it narrates a final supper with the disciples where the betrayal of Judas is predicted (13:26), it does not report any special words over the bread and wine. Instead, the focus is on Jesus washing the disciples' feet. Some have suggested that John is wishing to make a point about the sacraments, either a warning that they do not guarantee salvation (as in 1 Cor 10) or more positively, that those who were not present at the last supper have not missed out. This would fit with Jesus' reply to Thomas, 'Blessed are those who have not seen and yet have come to believe' (20:29). The Gospel is aiming to mediate an experience of Christ that is even greater than being originally present with him.

Secondly, instead of the agony of Gethsemane and Jesus' request that the cup might pass from him, John gives us four chapters of theological reflection on what later theology would call 'the persons of the Trinity'. Jesus is returning to the Father and the Father will send the Holy Spirit, who 'will teach you everything, and remind you of all that I have said to you' (14:26). The Holy Spirit is the 'Spirit of truth' (16:13), whom Jesus will send to 'guide you into all the truth'. Just as Jesus bore witness to the Father, so the Spirit will bear witness to Jesus, taking what is his and making it known to his disciples. This is brought to a tremendous climax in the prayer of John 17 (sometimes called the 'High Priestly Prayer'), where Jesus prays for himself, the disciples and those that will believe through their testimony:

> I glorified you on earth by finishing the work that you gave me to do. So now, Father, glorify me in your own presence with the glory that I had in your presence before the world existed... But now I am coming to you, and I speak these things in the world so that they may have my joy made complete in themselves... I ask not only on behalf of these, but also on behalf of those who will believe in me through their word, that they may all be one. As you, Father, are in me and I am in you, may they also be in us... (17:4–21; abbreviated)

Thirdly, when we return to the story of Jesus' passion, we are aware of a different focus. The emphasis is not on his suffering but how he is returning to the Father. Thus in the story of his arrest, when the guards come and ask for Jesus of Nazareth, he answers with the recognition formula *ego eimi* ('I am he'), whereby 'they stepped back and fell to the ground' (18:6). Thereafter, Jesus must take the initiative for his arrest (for Jesus must return to the Father). He asks them again, 'For whom are you looking?' and replies, 'I told you that I am he. So if you are looking for me, let these men go' (18:8). As Bultmann notes, this is not so much a request as an order. The disciples do not flee in John's Gospel; they are dismissed.

Fourthly, far from remaining silent before Pilate, Jesus almost teases him with his superior wisdom and insight. Pilate asks him, 'Are you the King of the Jews?' and Jesus replies, 'Do you ask this on your own, or did others tell you about me?' (18:34). So Pilate concludes that he is a king but Jesus replies, 'You say that I am a king. For this I was born, and for this I came into the world, to testify to the truth. Everyone who belongs to the truth listens to my voice' (18:37). Pilate can only reply, 'What is truth?' The earthly ruler is no match for the man from heaven.

Fifthly, instead of Mark's 'My God, my God, why have you forsaken me?' (Mark 15:34), John is much more like Luke, with three sayings from the cross, all of which are positive. The first urges his mother and the beloved disciple to look after one another (19:26–7). The second (19:28) is a request for a drink – not because he is in need but 'in order to fulfil the scripture' (what scripture is not clear). And the last saying, Jesus' final word from the cross before dying, is *tetelestai* ('It is finished'). Jesus has come into the world to do God's will and is now returning. Everything has gone according to plan.

Appendix (chapter 21)

The main reason for seeing this as an appendix is that chapter 20 seems to come to a natural conclusion: 'But these are written so that you may come to believe that Jesus is the Messiah, the Son of God, and that through believing you may have life in his name.' But then we have a further appearance to the disciples while they are out fishing (back in Galilee), a reinstatement of Peter, and a final claim for the reliability of the Gospel traditions. Of particular interest is the final dialogue between Jesus and Peter and the author's comment on this. Peter asks what will happen to the beloved disciple. Jesus replies, 'If it is my will that he remain until I come, what is that to you? Follow me!' The editor then feels the need to add the comment: 'So the rumour spread in the community that this disciple would not die. Yet Jesus did not say to him that he would not die, but, "If it is my will that he remain until I come, what is that to you?"' Some have concluded from this that it was the death of the 'beloved disciple' that precipitated the crisis that led to the production of the fourth Gospel.

John's portrait of Jesus

Divinity

The overwhelming impression that John's Gospel leaves is its emphasis on the divinity of Christ. Its opening sentence prepares us for this: 'In the beginning was the Word, and the Word was with God, and the Word was God. He was in the beginning with God.' That itself is not surprising. The author of Hebrews can call Jesus 'the reflection of God's glory and the exact imprint of God's very being' (1:3), and Colossians 1:19

says, 'For in him all the fullness of God was pleased to dwell.' What is surprising is that this exalted theology is found on the lips of Jesus himself. Thus in the dispute about healing the man at the pool on the Sabbath, Jesus does not argue (as in Mark 3:4) that it is surely better to do good on the Sabbath than evil. Rather, the argument is that since God is working on the Sabbath, so is Jesus (5:17), leading to a long discourse about the relationship between Father and Son (5:19–47). And according to the author of the Gospel, the point of controversy was that:

> for this reason the Jews were seeking all the more to kill him, because he was not only breaking the sabbath, but was also calling God his own Father, thereby making himself equal to God. (5:18)

In chapter 8, Jesus questions their claim to be Abraham's children with the accusation that they are really children of the devil (8:44). When they respond that he is the one who has a demon, Jesus says, 'Your ancestor Abraham rejoiced that he would see my day; he saw it and was glad' (8:56). The implication is not lost on them. They respond with the question, 'You are not yet fifty years old, and have you seen Abraham?' This gives Jesus the opportunity to declare, 'Very truly, I tell you, before Abraham was, I am (*ego eimi*)'. And if this is not clear enough, in another dispute, Jesus says, 'The Father and I are one' (10:30). The Gospel ends how it began, with an unequivocal declaration of the divinity of Christ, this time from the testimony of Thomas, who says, 'My Lord and my God!' (20:28).

Messiah

If Jesus knows of his pre-existence and divinity, he also knows of his role as Messiah and King. In the dialogue with the woman at the well (4:1–30), the woman confesses her own faith in the words, 'I know that Messiah is coming... When he comes, he will proclaim all things to us' (4:25). Jesus responds, 'I am he (*ego eimi*), the one who is speaking to you.' Indeed, though the disciples occasionally lose their way in John's Gospel (e.g. 4:31–3), they recognize the messiahship of Jesus at their very first meeting:

> One of the two who heard John speak and followed him was Andrew, Simon Peter's brother. He first found his brother Simon and said to him, 'We have found the Messiah.' (1:41)

> Jesus answered, 'I saw you under the fig tree before Philip called you.' Nathanael replied, 'Rabbi, you are the Son of God! You are the King of Israel!' (1:49)

Nevertheless, it is interesting that John does not subordinate messiahship ('God's anointed') to deity ('God's Son'). In Nathanael's reply above, the two affirmations are placed side by side, as they are in the purpose statement of 20:31: 'But these are written so that you may come to believe that Jesus is the Messiah, the Son of God, and that through believing you may have life in his name.' It does not appear to be John's purpose to elevate divinity above messiahship. The two belong together.

Eschatology

One of the most remarkable differences between John and the synoptic Gospels concerns eschatology. For apart from the occasional reference to the last day (6:40), the burden of Jesus' teaching in John is that those who believe in Jesus have eternal life here and now (e.g. 3:15,16, 36; 4:14,36; 5:24,39; 6:27,40,47,54,68). They are not waiting for a kingdom nor are they concerned about a coming judgement. Indeed, those who believe in Jesus will not be judged at all. They have passed from darkness to light. And though John does portray Jesus as predicting the destruction of the temple, the editorial aside tells us that actually 'he was speaking of the temple of his body' (2:21). The key phrase 'kingdom of God' (14 times in Mark, 32 times in Luke) and Matthew's equivalent 'kingdom of heaven' (32 times in Matthew) only occurs twice in John (3:3,5). If Luke has toned down the apocalyptic expectation of Mark, John has transformed it into something else. As Moody Smith says:

> The meaning of Jesus is not worked out against an apocalyptic, eschatological scheme, but rather the meaning of eschatology is redefined in light of the coming of Jesus. (1995, p. 106)

Humanity

Though the emphasis of John is undoubtedly on the divinity of Christ, there are several sayings which seem to emphasize his humanity. For example, he stops by the well because he was 'tired out by his journey' (4:6). He weeps by the grave of his friend Lazarus (11:35). At the crucifixion, one of the guards thrusts a spear into his side 'and at once blood and water came out' (19:34). And the word used for the incarnation in 1:14 is *sarx* ('flesh'). With all the emphasis on the oneness between Jesus and the Father, one might have expected a more personal word. But John says, 'And the Word became flesh'. Some have suggested that this might be a deliberate safeguard against the view that

Jesus only seemed to be human ('docetism'). It is certainly a concern in the Johannine epistles that anyone who does not acknowledge that Jesus came in the flesh is an 'antichrist' (1 John 4:2–3; 2 John 7).

Furthermore, while John's emphasis on the divinity of Christ is his most striking feature, the Gospel strongly emphasizes Jesus' obedience and subordination to the Father. Thus 'the Son can do nothing on his own, but only what he sees the Father doing' (5:19). The same applies to Jesus' teaching: 'I have not spoken on my own, but the Father who sent me has himself given me a commandment about what to say and what to speak' (12:49). Indeed, Jesus can even declare, 'the Father is greater than I' (14:28). Although John emphasizes the divinity of Christ, it is never as a rival to God the Father.

Interpretations of John's Gospel

Distorted history

As the title of his book suggests (*From Jewish Prophet to Gentile God*, 1991), Maurice Casey argues that the original picture of Jesus as a Jewish prophet has been changed into one of a Gentile God. Such a view, he says, would have been utterly impossible on Jewish presuppositions. When a man comes to Jesus in Mark's Gospel and says, 'Good Teacher', Jesus replies, 'Why do you call me good? No one is good but God alone' (10:18). But Gentiles were used to Greek and Roman stories of gods ascending and descending and so naturally used these to describe Jesus. He was with God; he came down; he went up. John is not writing history, he is distorting it. Jesus did not go around claiming to be God. He did not give four chapters of trinitarian theology in between the final meal with the disciples and his arrest. He did not continually speak about eternal life. He did not die in victorious confidence. These are changes made by the author in order to conform the narrative to his own theological viewpoint. Many will find this position extreme but it is a fact that those who try to reconstruct the 'historical Jesus' seldom include very much from John's Gospel. It is more often regarded as later theological reflection.

Distorted theology

Ernst Käsemann called John's Gospel 'naively docetic' (1968, p. 17), a story of 'God striding over the earth'. He acknowledges that the prologue speaks of incarnation ('And the Word became flesh') but believes this is completely swallowed up by the phrase that follows ('we have seen his glory'). John does not give us an account of a genuine human life (as one might expect from a genuine incarnation). Rather, the earthly life of Jesus is 'merely a backdrop for the Son of God proceeding through the world of man and as the scene of the in-breaking of the divine glory'. Far from the paradox that glory only comes through suffering, Jesus' death is simply his path back to the Father and the removal of those earthly limitations to which he occasionally submitted. It is no wonder that the second-century Gnostics took such a liking to John's Gospel. It was already moving in that direction.

A different history

If there is any truth in the above positions, one is bound to ask why the author bothered to use the narrative format at all. Why not simply write an epistle or a treatise setting out his theological beliefs? John Robinson (1985) argued that John had access to historical traditions that come from a different stream to those of the synoptic Gospels. For example, as a member of a pious family, it is entirely likely that Jesus visited Jerusalem for some of the major feasts. Luke has him attending as a youngster (2:41–52). Did he stop going when he was an adult? John's picture of Jesus ministering in Galilee but going up to Jerusalem for major feasts is actually very plausible.

Furthermore, it has been usual to dismiss John's chronology for being theologically motivated. For example, his placing of the death of Christ at the time when the Passover lambs were being slaughtered is clearly of significance (19:36). But equally, the synoptics' placing of the last supper to coincide with Passover (Luke 22:1) is also of theological significance. Historically speaking, which is right? Robinson argues for John's accuracy, for the synoptics themselves tell us that the Jewish leaders had decided *not* to arrest Jesus during the feast, lest there be a riot. But according to the synoptic chronology, this is precisely what they then go and do, whereas John has them arresting Jesus before the feast begins. Richard Bauckham thinks that John offers historical traditions that need to be combined with what we can learn from the synoptics (1998, pp. 147–71).

A type of theology

Clement of Alexandria (*c*. 200 CE) wrote that, 'last of all, aware that the physical facts had been recorded in the Gospels, encouraged by his pupils and irresistibly moved by the Spirit, John wrote a spiritual Gospel' (see Appendix). It is unlikely (from what else he says) that he thinks that John distorted the facts but it is clear that he regards John as in some ways different from the other Gospels. He has given us a spiritual or theological interpretation of the events as opposed to just narrating the facts (though modern scholars would no longer regard the synoptics thus). For example, all Christian believers think that the crucifixion was in some sense a victory, even though those present could only see disaster. But John is quite clear that later believers are in a far better position to understand what is going on than those who were actually present (2:22; 12:16; 20:9). Modern people, schooled in the Enlightenment, might prefer it if John had kept to the facts and then offered an interpretation, but it appears that he has fused them into a single theological narrative. As Marianne Thomson says:

> The differences between John and the Synoptics reflect different approaches to the best way to express the reality and significance of Jesus' person for those who believe... John means to tell the reader what, in his view, was really going on in what went on in the life of Jesus of Nazareth. (1996, pp. 33–4)

The fact that John has done this in the form of a narrative raises the question of legitimacy because countless believers have assumed that what they are reading is what actually happened. But if it is read as theological narrative, our acceptance or rejection of it is, in principle, no different from our acceptance or rejection of Paul or Hebrews. Schnackenburg claims that it 'reveals more of the will, the motives, and the inner driving powers that moved Jesus' (1995, p. 322). As a result, 'the historical dimension cannot be directly grasped but is still so experienceable that it does not produce dreams and fantasies' (1995, p. 322). The critical question is what we are to make of this 'image of Jesus' and the fact that the church has included it in its canon of scripture, along with the synoptic Gospels.

Conclusion

The question of history and theology has been with us throughout our study of the four Gospels. It was particularly raised by the changes that Matthew and Luke appear to have made to Mark. But it is most conspicuous when we compare John with the synoptics. There is no longer any reticence or ambiguity about Jesus. For John, the resurrection has proved that he was 'Son of God', and the whole story reflects that conclusion. The disciples recognized him as 'messiah' on their very first meeting. He openly proclaimed his relationship to the Father. He promised eternal life for believers, there and then. And he went confidently to his death, knowing that it was his return to the Father. The author of the Gospel is quite clear that he is offering an interpretation based on hindsight (2:22; 12:16; 20:9) and the inspiration of the Holy

Spirit (14:26). And it is an interpretation that proved very influential in the development of the creeds. Thus our study of the four Gospels raises two important questions:

1. Should we isolate the earliest material in the Gospels (if that is possible) and build our picture of Jesus on that alone?
2. Since all four Gospels combine history and hindsight (in a variety of ways), how are we to use them to understand the figure of Jesus?

Before we look at how modern scholars do use them, we will take a brief glimpse at what was being written about Jesus outside of Matthew, Mark, Luke and John – the so-called 'apocryphal gospels'.

6

Apocryphal gospels

Gospel of Thomas

Early church writers speak disparagingly of a *Gospel of Thomas*, but until 1945 its contents were unknown. Half a century earlier, various Greek fragments dated from about 200 CE had been found at Oxyrynchus in Egypt and occasionally received comment. But it was only through the discovery of the Coptic text at Nag Hammadi that these fragments were identified as part of the lost *Gospel of Thomas*. Perhaps because it was found among a whole series of heterodox texts, many of a gnostic flavour, early opinion regarded *Thomas* as a second-century distortion of the canonical Gospels (Grant and Freedman, 1960). But more recently, it has come to play an important role in Jesus research, for several reasons.

It contains parables that look primitive

Ever since Adolf Jülicher (1899) demonstrated the tendency of the second-century church to allegorize the parables, scholars have been suspicious of allegorical features in the synoptic parables. For example, the parable of the sower (Mark 4:3–9) is followed by an explanation of the four soils (4:13–20). Some scholars concluded that Mark or early church tradition had added this in order to draw out the meaning for a new audience. Other scholars replied that the explanation is in Matthew, Mark and Luke and there is no textual warrant for removing them. However, *Thomas* 9 contains a version of the parable that lacks the allegorical explanation. Did the author remove it or has he preserved a more original form than Mark?

Thomas 57 contains a version of the parable of the 'wheat and tares' which is less than half the length of Matthew's version (Matt 13:24–30, 36–43). If the two are compared, explanations like, 'The one who sows the good seed is the Son of Man' (Matt 13:37) and 'The Son of Man will send his angels' (Matt 13:41) look suspiciously like ecclesiastical additions (so Jeremias, 1972, pp. 81–5). *Thomas* 20 contains a simpler form of the mustard seed parable ('It is like a grain of mustard seed, smaller than all seeds. But when it falls on cultivated ground it puts forth a large branch and provides a shelter for the birds of heaven'). And in *Thomas* 65, there is a version of the parable of the vineyard which lacks many of the allegorical features found in Mark. For example, Mark's inclusion of the fence, pit, winepress and tower all make the allusion to Isaiah 5 more explicit. The father is to send his 'beloved son', an obvious reference to God's words at Jesus' baptism and transfiguration. And in Mark, not only are the tenants destroyed, the vineyard is given to others, providing an allusion to Gentile Christianity.

> A good man had a vineyard. He leased it to some farmers so that they would cultivate it and he would receive the fruit from them. He sent his servants so that the tenants would give him the fruit of the vineyard. They seized his servant, beat him and almost killed him. The servant returned and told his master. His master said, 'Perhaps they did not recognize him.' He sent another servant. The tenants beat him also. Then the master sent his son. He said, 'Perhaps they will respect my son.' Those tenants knowing he was the heir of the vineyard seized him and killed him. He who has ears, let him hear. Jesus said, 'Show me the stone which the builders rejected. That is the cornerstone.' (*Thomas* 65–66, text from Elliott's *The Apocryphal New Testament*, 1993)

It contains sayings that look primitive

Koester (1990, pp. 107–13) lists 27 sayings in *Thomas* that have parallels in Mark. Many of them are quite similar but a good case can be made for some of them being more primitive than Mark's version, which is generally longer:

> Jesus said, 'No prophet is acceptable in his own village; a physician does not heal those who know him.' (*Thomas* 31; cf. Mark 6:4–5)

> They showed Jesus a gold coin and said to him, 'Caesar's men demand taxes from us.' He said to them, 'Give to Caesar what belongs to Caesar; give to God what belongs to God, and give to me what is mine.' (*Thomas* 100; cf. Mark 12:14–16)

> The disciples said to him, 'Your brothers and your mother are standing outside.' He said to them, 'Those here who do the will of my

Father are my brothers and mother; it is they who will enter the kingdom of my Father.' (*Thomas* 99; cf. Mark 3:31–5)

Jesus said, 'It is impossible for anyone to enter the house of the strong
man and take it by force, unless he binds his hands; then he will be
able to pillage his house.' (*Thomas* 35; cf. Mark 3:25–7)

Its greatest affinity is with Q

Of the 79 sayings that *Thomas* has in common with the synoptic
Gospels, 46 of them come from Q, commonly regarded as earlier than
Mark (Koester, 1990, p. 87). Of particular interest are the parallels to
the sermon on the mount/plain. *Thomas* contains four beatitudes,
found in sayings 54, 68 and 69:

Blessed are the poor for yours is the kingdom of heaven. (54)

Blessed are you when you are hated and persecuted, and where you
have been persecuted they will find no place. (68)

Blessed are they who are persecuted in their heart; these are the ones
who have truly known the Father. Blessed are those who are hungry
for the belly of the needy will be filled. (69)

Matthew and Luke have much larger collections (Luke 6:20–3;
Matt 5:3–12) which, according to the majority of scholars, derive from
Q. If this is the case, then it is clear that both Luke and Matthew have
made certain changes to Q. For example, consider the beatitudes on
poverty and persecution:

Blessed are you who are poor, for yours is the kingdom of God.
(Luke 6:20)

Blessed are the poor *in spirit*, for theirs is the kingdom of heaven.
(Matt 5:3)

Blessed are you who are hungry now, for you will be filled. (Luke
6:21)

Blessed are those who hunger and thirst *for righteousness*, for they will
be filled. (Matt 5:6)

The difference between these two versions is that Luke imagines
Jesus to be talking about real poverty and hunger, whereas Matthew
thinks of it in religious terms. Which is the more original? The majority
of scholars think that Luke is closer to Q here and that Matthew has

introduced the theme of righteousness, as he does in the persecution saying ('Blessed are those who are persecuted *for righteousness' sake*'). But if that is the case, then *Thomas* proves more reliable than Matthew in preserving the original meaning of these sayings. Furthermore, in the saying about those who hate you, Matthew says 'on my account' (Matt 5:11) but Luke has 'on account of the Son of Man' (Luke 6:22). Now it may be that both of these go back to an original Aramaic saying which meant 'one such as I' and that explains the difference. But in terms of the Greek texts, Luke has Jesus using the phrase as a definite title, whereas Matthew does not. Which is more original? Most scholars would opt for Matthew's self-reference rather than Luke's explicit 'Son of Man' saying. But this is precisely what we find in *Thomas*, so in this instance, *Thomas* is closer to Jesus' words than Luke.

At the very least, all this should mean that *Thomas* deserves a hearing when trying to determine the most original form of Jesus' sayings (hence Funk and Hoover, 1993). However, two further points are necessary in order to understand the significance of *Thomas* for modern scholars. The first is made by Koester:

> One of the most striking features of the *Gospel of Thomas* is its silence on the matter of Jesus' death and resurrection – the keystone of Paul's missionary proclamation. But Thomas is not alone in this silence. The Synoptic Sayings Source (Q), used by Matthew and Luke, also does not consider Jesus' death a part of the Christian message. And it likewise is not interested in stories and reports about the resurrection and subsequent appearances of the risen Lord. The *Gospel of Thomas* and Q challenges the assumption that the early church was unanimous in making Jesus' death and resurrection the fulcrum of Christian faith. Both documents presuppose that Jesus' significance lay in his words, and in his words alone. (1990, p. 86)

This is an important conclusion. It suggests that not every branch of Christianity followed Paul and Mark in emphasizing Jesus' death above his teaching (see also the letter of James). Though we do not possess Q and some scholars doubt its existence, it is nevertheless true that Matthew and Luke both swing the emphasis more towards Jesus' teaching. And on some readings, Luke thinks of Jesus' death more as an exemplary martyrdom than as an atoning sacrifice. The accusation that Protestant Christianity reads Jesus through the lens of Paul (Sanders would say a misunderstanding of Paul) may have some truth to it.

The second point is more controversial. Many scholars who accept Q agree with Kloppenborg (1987) that Q has been subject to later redaction. In particular, it is the twin emphases on judgement falling on 'this generation' and the coming of the 'Son of Man' that are regarded

as later additions. This assessment of the evidence lies behind the portraits of Jesus found in Mack (1989) and Crossan (1991), who argue
that our earliest picture of Jesus is found in the parallels between
Thomas and the earliest strata of Q.

On the other hand, we should not ignore the esoteric nature of much
of *Thomas*. Some of its sayings have a distinctly world-denying (some
would say gnostic) feel to them. Its message appears to be 'individual
enlightenment', with nothing to say to society at large or to people living in community. Theissen (1998, p. 40) offers the following summary
of its key themes:

- *Jesus as revealer:* Jesus the living one is the bringer of salvation simply through his (several) words of revelation: 'Anyone who finds the
  interpretation of these words will not taste death' (logion 1).
- *Dualistic anthropology:* the world and with it the human body are
  devalued and become a synonym for death.
- *Present eschatology:* the kingdom... is an entity which is beyond time,
  the origin and goal of human beings who have come to know themselves.
- *Discipleship is achieved as turning away from the world:* the disciples
  are the individuals, the elect of the living Father, who are reached by
  the call of Jesus. A Christian community hardly comes into view
  here.

Gospel of Peter

In 1886–7, an eighth-century fragment of the *Gospel of Peter* was discovered at Akhmim in Egypt. As with *Thomas*, scholars originally saw it
as a second-century distortion of the canonical Gospels, but Crossan
believes it is based on the same source ('the cross gospel') which
underlies all the passion narratives. Certainly its use of the Old
Testament appears to be less sophisticated than in the canonical
Gospels. But it also contains some fantastic elements, such as Jesus
being led out of the tomb by two heavenly beings, a 'talking cross' and a
description of the risen Jesus whose head 'reached beyond the heavens'.
The fragment begins with Pilate washing his hands, and it seems intent
on exonerating him and blaming the Jews (Elliott, 1993, p. 151). It ends
with words supposedly from Peter: 'But we, the twelve disciples of the
Lord, wept and mourned and each one, grieving for what had happened, returned to his own home. But I, Peter, and my brother Andrew
took our nets and went to the sea' (60).

So they took the Lord and pushed him as they ran and said, 'Let us drag the Son of God along now that we have got power over him.' And they put upon him a purple robe and set him on the judgement seat... And they brought two malefactors and crucified the Lord between them. But he held his peace as (if) he felt no pain. And when they had set up the cross they wrote: 'This is the King of Israel.' And having laid down his garments before him they divided them among themselves and cast lots for them. But one of the malefactors rebuked them saying, 'We are suffering for the deeds which we have committed, but this man, who has become the saviour of men, what wrong has he done you?' And they were angry with him and commanded that his legs should not be broken so that he might die in torment. (6–14)

Now it was midday and darkness covered all Judea. And they became anxious and distressed lest the sun had already set since he was still alive. It stands written for them: 'The sun should not set on one that has been murdered.' And one of them said, 'Give him to drink gall with vinegar... And many went about with lamps (and) as they supposed that it was night, they stumbled. And the Lord called out and cried, 'My power, O power, you have forsaken me!' And having said this, he was taken up. And at the same hour the veil of the temple in Jerusalem was torn in two. (15–20)

But the scribes and Pharisees and elders... were afraid and came to Pilate, entreating him and saying, 'Give us soldiers that we may guard his sepulchre for three days, lest his disciples come and steal him away and the people suppose that he is risen from the dead, and do us harm... Early in the morning, when the Sabbath dawned, there came a crowd from Jerusalem and the country round about to see the sealed sepulchre. Now in the night in which the Lord's day dawned... there was a loud voice in heaven, and they saw the heavens open and two men come down from there in a great brightness and draw near to the sepulchre. That stone which had been laid against the entrance to the sepulchre started of itself to roll and move sidewards, and the sepulchre was opened and both young men entered. When those soldiers saw this, they awakened the centurion and the elders, for they also were there to mount guard. And while they were narrating what they had seen, they saw three men come out from the sepulchre, two of them supporting the other and a cross following them and the heads of the two reaching to heaven, but that of him who was being led reached beyond the heavens. And they heard a voice out of the heavens crying, 'Have you preached to those who sleep?', and from the cross there was heard the answer, 'Yes.' (28–42)

Infancy gospels

As we have seen, Matthew and Luke felt the need to prefix the story of Jesus with a brief account of his birth and one story about his childhood (Luke). Some scholars regard these as legends but they are fairly sober compared with what was to follow. Infancy narratives flourished in the second and third centuries, the most famous being the *Protoevangelium of James*. There are over 100 extant Greek manuscripts of this document and translations into Syriac, Ethiopic, Georgian, Sahidic, Slavonic and Armenian (Elliott, 1993, p. 48). *The Gospel of Pseudo-Matthew* supplies additional proof-texts for the flight to Egypt and return to Nazareth, while *The Infancy Gospel of Thomas* (no connection with the *Gospel of Thomas*) provides stories of Jesus' childhood. What is surprising about the latter is that the child prodigy also has a dark side, wreaking vengeance on those who oppose him. The following extracts have been arranged chronologically, according to subject matter:

> In the ninth month Anna gave birth. And she said to the midwife, 'What have I brought forth?' And she said, 'A female.' And Anna said, 'My soul is magnified this day.' And when the days were completed, Anna purified herself and gave suck to the child, and called her Mary. Day by day the child grew strong; when she was six months old her mother stood her on the ground to see if she could stand. And she walked seven steps and came to her bosom. And she took her up saying, 'As the Lord my God lives, you shall walk no more upon this earth until I bring you into the temple of the Lord.' And she made a sanctuary in her bedroom and did not permit anything common or unclean to pass through it. (*Protoevangelium* 5:2 – 6:1)

> And when the child was three years old (Joachim) placed her on the third step of the altar, and the Lord God put grace upon her and she danced with her feet, and the whole house of Israel loved her... And Mary was in the temple of the Lord nurtured like a dove and received food from the hand of an angel... And the priest said to Joseph, 'You have been chosen by lot to receive the virgin of the Lord as your ward. But Joseph answered him, 'I have sons and am old; she is but a girl.' ... And the priest said to Joseph, 'Fear the Lord your God.' ... And Joseph was afraid and received her as his ward. (*Protoevangelium* 7:2 – 9:2)

> Now when she was in her sixth month... Joseph entered his house and found her with child. And he struck his face, threw himself down on the ground on sackcloth and wept bitterly... And the priest said,

'You have consummated your marriage in secret... I will give you both to drink the water of the conviction of the Lord, and it will make your sins manifest...' And the priest took it and gave it to Joseph to drink and sent him into the hill-country, and he returned whole. And he made Mary drink also, and sent her into the hill-country, and she returned whole. And all the people marvelled, because sin did not appear in them. And the priest said, 'If the Lord God has not revealed your sins, neither do I judge you.' (*Protoevangelium* 13:1 – 16:1)

And on the third day after the birth of our Lord Jesus Christ, Mary went out of the cave and, entering a stable, placed the child in the manger, and an ox and an ass adored him. Then was fulfilled that which was said by Isaiah the prophet, 'The ox knows his owner, and the ass his master's crib.' ... And on the journey there were with Joseph three boys, and with Mary a girl. And behold, suddenly there came out of the cave many dragons; and when the boys saw them they cried out in great terror. Then Jesus got down from his mother's lap and stood on his feet before the dragons; and they worshipped Jesus and then departed. Then was fulfilled that which was said by David the prophet, 'Praise the Lord from the earth, dragons, and all you ocean depths.' (*Pseudo-Matthew* 14, 18)

When this boy Jesus was five years old he was playing at the crossing of a stream, and he gathered together into pools the running water, and instantly made it clean... Having made soft clay he moulded from it twelve sparrows. And it was the sabbath... Joseph cried out... 'Why do you do on the sabbath things which it is not lawful to do?' But Jesus clapped his hands and cried out to the sparrows and said to them, 'Be gone!' And the sparrows took flight and went away chirping... After this he again went through the village, and a child ran and knocked against his shoulder. Jesus was angered and said to him, 'You shall not go further on your way', and immediately he fell down and died... When he was six years old, his mother gave him a pitcher and sent him to draw water and bring it into his house. But in the crowd he stumbled, and the pitcher was broken. But Jesus spread out the garment he was wearing, filled it with water and brought it to his mother. (*Infancy Gospel of Thomas* 2, 4, 11)

His father was a carpenter... and received an order from a rich man to make a bed for him. But when one beam was shorter than its corresponding... Jesus stood at the other end and took hold of the shorter piece of wood, and stretching it made it equal to the other. (*Infancy Gospel of Thomas* 13)

And when he was twelve years old his parents went according to the custom to Jerusalem... And while they were returning, the child Jesus went back to Jerusalem... they found him in the temple sitting among the teachers, listening and asking them questions. And all paid attention to him and marvelled how he, a child, put to silence the elders and teachers of the people, elucidating the chapters of the law and the parables of the prophets... But the scribes and Pharisees said, 'Are you the mother of this child?' And she said, 'I am.' And they said to her, 'Blessed are you among women, because God has blessed the fruit of your womb. For such glory and such excellence and wisdom we have never seen nor heard.' (*Infancy Gospel of Thomas* 19)

Unlike the *Gospel of Thomas*, almost all scholars believe that these accounts are late and fill in the gaps left by the canonical Gospels. They do not, therefore, add anything to our knowledge of the historical Jesus. But that does not mean that they are unimportant. For one thing, some would say that they are only continuing the trend begun by Matthew and Luke and finding full expression in John. They are not to be dismissed simply because they contain later reflection. Later reflection may contain genuine insights that were hidden from those that were 'too close' to the events.

Furthermore, these Gospels show us the sort of pictures of Jesus that were being propagated in the second and third centuries. And these centuries were of crucial significance in the development of doctrine. For example, the controversy of whether Mary should properly be called 'God-bearer' (which was accepted by the majority) is undoubtedly illuminated by the texts above. And as church history shows, it has greatly influenced the way that Jesus has been regarded.

One of the characteristics of the modern study of Jesus is its use of a variety of extra-canonical material. Some of it, like *Thomas*, may contain actual sayings of Jesus. Other texts, such as the Dead Sea Scrolls, Jewish apocalypses, wisdom collections and secular papyri are all used to provide an appropriate context for understanding Jesus. The view that nothing outside the Bible is relevant to an understanding of Jesus is now a minority position. Scholars of all persuasions regularly use texts from outside the Bible to inform their study, even if it is still true that the majority give pre-eminence to the canonical books. How they go about that task is the theme of the rest of this book.

7

Jesus: prophet of doom?

In Chapters 2–6 we looked at the canonical Gospels, and at a selection of the non-canonical material, to gain an impression of their main emphases and differences. However, when the figure of Jesus is interpreted, whether as a historical person, as an inspiration for ethics or art, or as a stimulus for religious belief, people do not usually turn to just one of these Gospels. Even if one or two of the Gospels may prove to be more influential than others on a person's understanding of Jesus, material from the other Gospels is usually combined to create the resulting picture. Furthermore, if one Gospel becomes dominant, that is rarely through conscious choice. The way that Gospels influence readers often goes unrecognized. Historians are more likely to take note of which Gospel or Gospels they use most, for they will be seeking the most reliable source. But this seldom means elevating one Gospel above all others. The results of form criticism suggest that each story needs to be examined on its own merits.

Pictures of Jesus, then, are always likely to draw from a number of the Gospels. As such, these pictures will always be selective. Our task in these next chapters is to examine the ways in which the Gospels have been read and used by modern scholars in constructing their picture of the historical Jesus. In this chapter, we will consider those scholars that opt for an eschatological portrait of Jesus. The second main track, describing Jesus as an itinerant wisdom teacher, will be dealt with in the next chapter. And in Chapter 9, we will consider a number of scholars whose views do not fit easily within these two main categories.

The impact of Schweitzer

Some say it's all Albert Schweitzer's fault. Schweitzer's *The Quest of the Historical Jesus*, which first appeared as *Von Reimarus zu Wrede* (1906), surveyed the many attempts from Reimarus (1778) to Wrede (1901) to uncover the 'Jesus of history'. After offering his lengthy, but exhilarating, journey through past efforts, Schweitzer then added his own. It was a landmark in the modern study of Jesus. Even though most of its features were far from original, his account has sent reverberations through New Testament study, and through all efforts to try to understand the historical figure of Jesus, ever since.

In a nutshell, Schweitzer was saying that Jesus was essentially a prophet of doom. The end was nigh and Jesus thought that God was going to break into history in his own lifetime. When this did not happen, Jesus initially thought he had made a mistake. But his mistake was not the conclusion that the end was coming soon. Rather, it was his failure to realize that he himself was to play the decisive role in bringing this about. So the events in Jerusalem which led to his crucifixion are to be understood as Jesus' attempt to hasten the end and allow God's kingdom to overtake human history.

Schweitzer brought to the forefront of modern scholarship the sheer distance and strangeness of the figure we are studying. Or, to put it a different way, by showing just how important eschatology was for Jesus, Schweitzer presents us with a Jesus who does not fit easily within most people's interpretations (spiritual example, wise teacher, ethical guide, divine envoy, political agitator). In order to explore this, we need to ask what Jesus meant when he spoke about the kingdom. What was it that he expected to happen soon?

Jesus and the kingdom

As Schweitzer shows, many nineteenth-century portraits of Jesus simply tried to make him too contemporary, so that he could function as a confirmation or corrective of the theology of the time. The pictures of Jesus then being propagated were suspiciously similar to the religious values of their authors. The Gospels were being read selectively, and important aspects of the evidence were being overlooked. But in 1892, Johannes Weiss published a brief but influential study called *Jesus' Proclamation of the Kingdom of God* (finally translated into English in 1971). Weiss realized that even though people were ready to talk about Jesus and about his preaching of the kingdom of God, some of what was actually contained in the Gospels about that kingdom (and in particular when that kingdom was to come) was being ignored. Weiss therefore set about a detailed study of the Gospel evidence, drawing the results of his enquiry together in a series of ten conclusions. Here are some of his key statements (1971, pp.129-30):

1. Jesus' activity is governed by the strong and unwavering feeling that the messianic time is imminent...

2. [The] actualization of the Kingdom of God has yet to take place...
   The disciples were to pray for the coming of the Kingdom of God,
   but men (sic) could do nothing to establish it.

3. Not even Jesus can bring, establish, or found the Kingdom of God;
   only God can do so...

5. Although Jesus initially hoped to live to see the establishment of the
   Kingdom, he gradually became certain that before this could happen, he must cross death's threshold... the coming of the Kingdom
   cannot be determined in advance by observation of signs or calcula-
   tion...

8. The land of Palestine will arise in a new and glorious splendor,
   forming the center of the new Kingdom.

Weiss does not wholly overlook the fact, even in his concluding
statements, that in the canonical Gospels there is a sense in which the
kingdom of God *has already* broken into history. But it is clear, particularly from statement 2, just where his emphasis lies. He also noted the
ignorance of Jesus (Jesus himself does not know when the end will
come), the limited power of Jesus (he cannot bring about the end), and
the 'this-worldliness' of the kingdom of God (the solid earth of
Palestine will be the focal point). One final aspect is worth highlighting:
Weiss's account shares with Schweitzer's an emphasis on the conviction
that Jesus thought he was achieving something by dying.

This last point may sound strange to readers used to seeing the
Gospels through the lens of later Christian interpretation. But it is by
no means obvious from the Gospels alone that Jesus deliberately went
to Jerusalem to 'usher in the kingdom' or 'make atonement for sin' or
'reconcile humanity to God'. Whatever Christian interpretation has
made of Jesus' death (Christians would say 'rightly made'), historically
it may simply have been a gross miscarriage of justice. He may have
been unwilling to die (Mark 14:34). He may have had no specific plans
to cause a disturbance when he went up to Jerusalem (which may have
been the first and only time he went to Jerusalem, or the last of a number of visits). In highlighting this point, as a link between Weiss and
Schweitzer, we are illustrating just what kind of challenge is entailed in
trying to separate out 'Jesus' and 'the Gospels'. Trying to find out about
Jesus in and through the Gospels, but only reading them with Christian
eyes (i.e. within the context of the New Testament, understood as scripture, and in relation to church life, past and present), can prevent us
from asking some key questions, the answer to which might prove
(ironically) profoundly important for Christianity.

Both Weiss and Schweitzer were Christians. They did not set out to be critical of Christianity in any way. They each believed that they were being 'more historical' in their respective readings of the canonical Gospels. Though we shall see in the final chapter of this book that a simple polarity of Christian/theological versus historical readings of Jesus and the Gospels cannot be maintained, it is clear that the attempt to try to locate the Jesus of history is going to have theological implications. It is, in other words, always likely to make Christians, and perhaps Jews too, 'think again' about Jesus.

The Weiss-Schweitzer approach to the study of Jesus was revolutionary. The new (or rediscovered) picture of Jesus as eschatological prophet dealt a critical blow to the more easily accessible, comfortable images of Jesus which were being offered in late nineteenth/early twentieth-century Europe. It sent people scurrying to the Gospels themselves to see if the picture was right. And it is a picture which has found supporters ever since. In the present day, one of its most eloquent and authoritative supporters is E.P. Sanders, the American New Testament scholar. In two books, a weighty scholarly volume *Jesus and Judaism* (1985) and a smaller, more popular, text *The Historical Figure of Jesus* (1993), Sanders offers a clear portrayal of Jesus as a Jewish prophet with a keen awareness of his own personal significance for the coming of God's kingdom. Crucial to Sanders' approach is a comprehensive study of first-century Judaism (on which Sanders is an authority), which enables us to locate Jesus within a plausible religious world. Sanders' conclusion is that Jesus fits within 'Jewish restoration eschatology'.

Sanders' enquiries lead him to regard Jesus as a prophet who sees the kingdom as future but imminent, his own role that of enabling Israel to be gloriously reconstituted by God in the near future. His resulting picture of Jesus is thus similar to that of Weiss and Schweitzer in stressing the eschatological dimension of Jesus' preaching, teaching and wider ministry, and in focusing upon the historical Israel. Sanders has a rather different explanation of the death of Jesus, viewing it as a piece of political intrigue resulting from the offence Jesus caused to the Jerusalem authorities. He therefore does not fall into line with the view that Jesus somehow *intended* to die on the trip to Jerusalem, as if he sensed that he had to offer himself in order for the end to occur. Sanders thus adheres more firmly to the view that the future, and the kingdom, really are God's alone. But his picture of Jesus is nevertheless sufficiently close to that of Weiss and Schweitzer for us to draw them alongside each other and class them as what we may call the first of two major tendencies, or trajectories, in the study of the historical Jesus.

Eschatology and the Gospels

Is the Weiss-Schweitzer-Sanders approach a plausible reading of the Gospels? The first thing to note is that support for it rests largely on evidence found in the synoptic Gospels. The fourth Gospel is usually left out of the picture here. This is significant, as there are few miracles mentioned in John's Gospel (and certainly no exorcisms), the kingdom of God gets scant mention, and it contains no parables. Yet it is through healings and miracles, and especially exorcisms, that the eschatological activity of Jesus is seen to be evident. And so much of the support for Jesus' proclamation of an imminent end to the present order of things is based on an understanding of the term 'kingdom of God'. A judgement of some kind is therefore being made by supporters of this view that the synoptic Gospels have somehow got Jesus 'more right' (historically speaking) than John. But on what is such a judgement based? Which particular parts of the synoptic Gospels are being leant upon? And are there any aspects of the synoptic portrayal of Jesus, let alone that of John or the non-canonical Gospels, that are being overlooked?

Let us begin with Schweitzer. Central to his understanding of Jesus is the material found in Matthew 10. What, he asks, lay behind Jesus' sending out of the twelve disciples? Schweitzer is quite clear:

> the whole of the discourse at the sending forth of the Twelve, taken in the clear sense of the words, is a prediction of the events of the 'time of the end,' events which are immediately at hand, in which the supernatural eschatological course of history will break through into the natural course. (1954, p. 360)

The mission of the twelve is seen as a last-ditch preaching campaign, summoning all to prepare for the End. This is the lynch-pin of Schweitzer's argument. But lots of other material gathers round it. Schweitzer reads the suffering predictions, found prominently in Mark, as an aspect of the eschatological expectation which Jesus embodied in his preaching and teaching. He understands the temptation element within the Lord's Prayer (Matt 6:13; Luke 11:4) also as an eschatological motif. And the apparent attempts of Jesus to escape the crowds (Mark 6:30–3) are read by Schweitzer as indicators that Jesus wanted to be with his disciples to await the coming of the kingdom. Schweitzer considers both the baptism and the last supper to be eschatological events. Jesus headed for Jerusalem to compel the kingdom of God to come, aware that he had to give up his life for 'many' (Mark 10:45; 14:24).

Crucial for Schweitzer's argument is his reading of Jewish apocalyptic literature (e.g. Daniel, Enoch, Psalms of Solomon). It is within the framework of such texts, claims Schweitzer, that early Christianity emerged. 'What else, indeed, are the Synoptic Gospels, the Pauline letters, the Christian apocalypses than products of Jewish apocalyptic, belonging... to its greatest and most flourishing period?' (1954, pp. 365–6). What Schweitzer is doing, then, is noting the importance of eschatological fervour in first-century Judaism, and reading the figure of Jesus through it:

> The self-consciousness of Jesus cannot... be illustrated or explained; all that can be explained is the eschatological view, in which the Man who possessed that self-consciousness saw reflected in advance the coming events, both those of a more general character, and those which especially related to Himself. (1954, p. 365)

Furthermore, Schweitzer's assumption that Matthew's Gospel was the first to be written (and, as we noted in Chapter 3, was the most Jewish of the Gospels), itself shapes his understanding of Jesus.

Schweitzer is not obviously wrong on either count: what Judaism was like at the time of Jesus will clearly prove crucial for what Jesus himself was like; the earliest Gospel to have been written is likely to 'play the lead role' in any interpretation (certainly any historical interpretation) of Jesus. However, he is not obviously right either, and we shall need to assess his conclusions both in this chapter and in later chapters. We can, however, note the value of two points: we have to be clear where both Jesus and the Gospels fit within Judaism; and we need to be clear which Gospel we think was written first, and what we do with that conclusion. On the first point, saying Jesus was 'a Jew' is not enough. What type of Jew was he? (Thoroughly obedient? Loyal? Critical? Provincial? Jerusalem-centred?) Did he have close links with any particular party? (Sadducees? Pharisees? Scribes? Zealots? Essenes?) Was he critical of any particular Jewish tradition because he was closest to it, or because he was more distant from it? On the second point, how do we know that we possess historically reliable information, even if we believe we have located the first Gospel to be written?

Schweitzer's drawing attention to the importance of Jewish apocalyptic links him directly with Weiss before him and Sanders after him. Weiss's exposition of 'the coming transformation' and the nature of the judgement which will accompany the arrival of the (imminently future) kingdom of God finds him dipping into the books of 4 Ezra and Enoch to set up the context for such passages as Mark 13:24–5. The cataclysmic events which are anticipated in such texts in turn provide the context for Weiss's reading of passages in which Jesus seems to refer to a new heaven and a new earth (Matt 19:28; Mark 14:25). With regard to judgement, Weiss admits that it is unclear from the Gospels whether

Jesus believed that those who are to be condemned as a result of the final judgement will be annihilated or subjected to eternal torment, for Mark 8:35 seems to contradict Matthew 25:41,46 (Weiss, 1971, p. 99). It is, however, clear that the judgement and the kingdom's coming are directly linked (Mark 9:43–8). If the kingdom is coming soon, then judgement is, too.

Despite the common ground between Weiss and Schweitzer in locating Jesus and the Gospels within the tradition of Jewish apocalyptic literature, they differ in one significant respect: Weiss believed Mark was the first Gospel to have been written. He does not, though, take Mark wholly at face value. For he thinks that the chronological order of the material in Mark may be historically inaccurate (see Appendix). This difference between Weiss and Schweitzer, though, indicates that support for the first Gospel to be written will be influential, but not necessarily decisive, in the quest for a historically accurate picture of Jesus. Other factors (in particular, the understanding of what part of Judaism Jesus fits into) always come into play. In any case, as we saw in the opening chapter, historical conclusions about Jesus are not all that the Gospels are interested in. We shall return to such matters later in the book.

E.P. Sanders supports Mark as the first Gospel to be written. His use of the Gospels, however, finds him traversing the whole synoptic material, picking up his evidence piece by piece. Sanders is clearly a scholar who operates after the form critics, his work thoroughly informed by the conviction that you have to take each story and saying on its own merits. Unlike so many studies of the Gospels, though, Sanders prefers to focus on the actions, rather than on the sayings, of Jesus. His reasoning is simple: you can't put too much weight on odd turns of phrase which are not even preserved in Jesus' first language. It is better to try to find out what Jesus *did*, in order to make sense of him. Even so:

> If we calmly survey all of the kingdom sayings, we shall see that most of them place the kingdom *up there*, in heaven, where people will enter after death, and *in the future*, when God brings the kingdom to earth and separates the sheep from the goats. (1993, p. 176)

In other words, the kingdom is of God and is in the future. But, claims Sanders, the actions of Jesus demonstrate this even more firmly than the sayings, which in any case seem to point clearly in that direction.

Like Weiss and Schweitzer, Sanders is keen to locate Jesus clearly within his Jewish milieu and suggests that this is an apocalyptic trajectory, from John the Baptist to early eschatologically minded Christianity (1 Thess 4:16–17). But Sanders is less impressed than earlier scholars about the value of trying to prove that first-century Jews expected a divine 'Son of God' or 'Son of Man' to appear. Rather, without doubting that early Christians made rapid links between Jesus' miracle-working, his evident lofty self-claims, and currently available titles of dignity, Sanders prefers to focus upon all the events from the life of Jesus which he can conclude actually happened (with the greatest degree of probability, that is). Together they suggest that Jesus made sense of his own life in terms of the imminently arriving kingdom of God.

Like most contemporary scholars, Sanders makes much of the miracles, and stresses the importance of seeing them in their first-century context. Problematic though they may be for interpreters today, in first-century terms although striking they are not so extraordinary that those who perform them should be regarded as divine (see Matt 12:27). What is more, the significance of Jesus' miraculous actions would be seen as signals of the eschatological time only by those who were already 'in the know'.

Much more significant for Sanders is a series of actions through which Jesus seems to place himself firmly within (and possibly at the end of) the prophetic tradition. The gathering of 'the twelve' (even if the precise twelve cannot be listed without difficulty) is one such act. The significance of the number was not lost on Matthew, who has Jesus saying to the disciples, 'you who have followed me will also sit on twelve thrones, judging the twelve tribes of Israel' (19:28). On the way to Jerusalem, Jesus performs three actions which can each be regarded as prophetic. First, he rides into Jerusalem on an ass, fulfilling, according to Matthew, the prophecy of Zechariah 9:9. Secondly, he overturns the tables of the money-changers in the temple, although there is debate as to precisely what he was objecting to. And thirdly, he shares a significant meal with his closest friends and allies, which, according to the synoptic Gospels, coincided with the Passover meal.

Sanders is therefore looking for signs within the activity of Jesus which indicate who he thought he was, and what he thought he was doing. He admits that Jesus seems to subvert some of what would be expected of an eschatological prophet. Jesus is interested in sinners, repentance and judgement. But though he has close contact with sinners, he does not appear to require them to repent first. He does want people to behave better than they do; indeed, says Sanders, he is something of a moral perfectionist. However:

> He did not... address a message to Israel to the effect that at the end there would be a great assize at which Israel would be vindicated and the nations rebuked and destroyed; and it seems that he did not make thematic the message that Israel should repent and mend their ways

so as to escape punishment at the judgment. (1985, p. 115)

Though Jesus is to be understood eschatologically, parts of the Gospels show that early Christianity had not quite understood Jesus' particular brand of 'restoration eschatology'. The 'summary text' of Mark 1:15 is, says Sanders, misleading. Repentance was not the hall-mark of Jesus' proclamation of the kingdom of God in the way it had been for John the Baptist.

For Sanders, then, Jesus is a radically consistent Jew, whose respect for the law was such that 'we should be very hesitant to accept the com-mon view of New Testament scholars that he had actually opposed the Jewish law' (1993, p. 224). Most of the cases where Jesus is alleged to have broken the Jewish law (Mark 2:1–12,23–8; 3:1–6; 7:1–23) prove to be nothing of the sort, either because they are unlikely to have hap-pened as written, or because they assume a law has been broken when it has not. Sanders admits to 'two points where Jesus asserted his own authority' – the commandment to 'let the dead bury their own dead' (Matt 8:21–2) and his calling of sinners, already mentioned. But these do not constitute the wholesale rejection of the law which is commonly assumed. Rather, Jesus' place within Judaism is as a person who had a high self-claim, precisely because he saw that the future transformation by God of the present world order was imminent. Far from a rejection of Judaism, this was Judaism's fulfilment, and Israel's restoration. The end was indeed nigh.

A provisional assessment

From this first, extended look at one composite image of Jesus (the Weiss-Schweitzer-Sanders trajectory), we are confronted with an inevitable circle of interpretation, which is always the case when we try to understand a historical figure. A basic picture is used to read the texts, yet it is the texts which have supplied the picture in the first place. That particular circle must either be entered at some point, and fol-lowed round, or it must be broken, and an alternative put in its place. But we must note the merits and impact of this image of Jesus before suggesting ways in which it might be mistaken.

Its main merit is its strong attempt to place Jesus appropriately within first-century Judaism. In other words, this line of interpretation is most likely to respect Jesus' strangeness (which arises from his sheer historical distance from us) and to resist the tendency to accept too easily certain Christian assumptions about Jesus, merely because the primary texts are themselves Christian.

Secondly, this picture of Jesus is based on a critical evaluation of the

Gospel material. In particular, it builds on the critical consensus that the most reliable material is found in Mark and Matthew. Weiss, Schweitzer and Sanders disagree as to which Gospel came first but they all agree that Mark and Matthew should take pride of place in any historical reconstruction. Thus these scholars would claim that they have not simply 'opted' for an eschatological portrait of Jesus. It is the dominant image in our earliest and most reliable sources. However, as we have already noted, not all scholars would agree with this judgement.

Thirdly, as Sanders stresses, we have a picture of Jesus which seems to make sense of how the John the Baptist movement could have become Pauline Christianity, via Jesus. When the emergence of early Christianity is viewed in that way, it is difficult to conclude that Jesus was anything but an eschatological figure, and that he thought of himself as such, and spoke and acted accordingly.

We must, though, note some possible problems. First, we must ask whether eschatological expectation was quite so fervent at the time of Jesus as this theory seems to presuppose. Although most textbooks on 'Judaism at the time of Jesus' readily map out a range of hopes about the future within Judaism, it is not clear any tradition of expectation was dominant. Nor is it certain that Jesus can be linked easily with one particular strand of eschatological expectation. As John Riches states:

> Jesus certainly looked for some imminent act of intervention on God's part... I am doubtful whether he, any more than John the Baptist, spelled that out in very full terms. The Gospels certainly do. (1990, p. 104)

In other words, an affirmation that Jesus expected God to act does not easily translate into the fine detail of how Jesus understood that action. Schweitzer, for one, may be reading Matthew's own interpretation of the eschatology of Jesus rather too quickly as if it were Jesus' own. Furthermore, it is quite possible that Schweitzer himself may have been caught up in 'end of century' fever at the time when he was re-assessing the rather tame Jesuses proposed by the scholars before him.

A second question about this eschatological reading of Jesus arises from what we mean by 'eschatology' and 'apocalyptic'. A number of scholars recently have questioned the ease with which 'apocalyptic' becomes linked with a sort of other-worldly cataclysmic event (Wright, 1992, 1996; Borg and Wright, 1998). Although this may highlight Jesus' strangeness to late twentieth/early twenty-first century ears, it may also lead us astray. 'Apocalyptic', after all, simply means the revelation of that which was hidden. Jesus may well have believed himself to have a significant role in God's ultimate self-revelation. 'Ultimacy' thus reflects the apparent eschatological dimension in Jesus' teaching and doing: his speech and acts are crucial events. But 'other-worldliness' may not be in his mind at all. His reference to a coming kingdom of God might have little to do with an imminent series of cataclysmic events. Thus our wrestling with the Gospels may be a matter of trying to disentangle an admittedly eschatological message from a crassly literal interpretation of it. As we shall see in our next chapter, that is precisely what many contemporary scholars do think.

In this regard, Wright's work is especially interesting. His conclusions about Jesus logically place him in this chapter. For Wright, it is clear that Jesus is an eschatological figure. With Jesus, the end has come. This means that all that Israel had hoped for was coming to fulfilment in and through the words and actions of Jesus: the return from exile was happening (Wright, 1996, pp. 249,268); evil was being defeated (pp. 243,461,481); Yahweh was returning to Zion (pp. 204–6, 463,481). But Wright's re-defining of apocalyptic in 'this-worldly' terms, which he claims to be more true to first-century meanings, enables him to construct a picture of Jesus who is both eschatological and also rooted within the socio-political climate of first-century Palestine.

This line of questioning does not, then, necessarily oppose an eschatological understanding of Jesus. It merely forces us to say more precisely what we mean by it. It may be that the particular eschatological fervour 'discovered' by Weiss and Schweitzer belongs more to the early church (1 Cor 7:29–31; 1 Thess 4:15) than to Jesus.

A third angle of questioning invites a direct counter to Sanders' method. Even granted Sanders' point that you shouldn't read too much into the odd Greek word, what if Sanders' emphasis upon actions over sayings has led him to play down the significance of Jesus' apparently being a teacher of some kind? Or what if some of the more incidental, routine actions of Jesus, such as breaking social taboos, suggests a strategy of social subversion rather than apocalyptic destruction? Perhaps Jesus' understanding of the imminent action of God in human history (the coming of the kingdom of God), though thoroughly Jewish in form and content, was highly original and has to be understood in the light of *all* that Jesus said and did.

Beyond the Weiss-Schweitzer-Sanders axis

Of course, in no way should this eschatological reading of Jesus be seen as the sole way in which 'Jesus within Judaism' should be understood. Geza Vermes sees strong similarities between Jesus and Galilean holy men of the same period (Vermes, 1973, 1983, 1993). Richard Horsley wants us to look at the wider political ramifications of Judaism at the time of Jesus, to prevent our viewing the 'religion' of Judaism too narrowly in late twentieth-century terms (Horsley 1987, 1994). Like Vermes and Horsley, Freyne (1988, 1994) explores the importance of Galilee (as opposed to Jerusalem) as the context within which Jesus is to be understood. It would therefore be quite wrong for us to assume that readings of Jesus which focus strongly upon his position within Judaism inevitably produce a starkly eschatological figure. As we shall see in the next chapter, there are other possibilities.

8

Jesus: witty word-spinner?

We ended the previous chapter noting that questions can be raised about understanding Jesus primarily as an eschatological figure. In this chapter, we examine a different interpretation of Jesus. This stresses the way in which Jesus focuses upon *this* world (which he seeks to transform) rather than on any kind of apocalyptic future. In some versions of this interpretation, Jesus' role as teacher is highlighted over that of prophet. However, this 'trajectory' of interpretation will be a much looser alliance than was possible in the previous chapter.

Jesus the peasant Jewish Cynic

To turn from the work of Weiss, Schweitzer and Sanders to that of the contemporary biblical scholar John Dominic Crossan is to enter a different world. In a number of books written over many years (but, for our purposes, especially in 1991 and 1994), Dominic Crossan has been offering an interpretation of Jesus and the early Christian movement which challenges many long-held assumptions about Christianity's origins. At the heart of Crossan's exposition is a view of Jesus as a 'peasant Jewish Cynic'. We must therefore begin by appreciating the full force of each of these terms as Crossan understands them, before going on to note how he has reached his conclusions.

Peasant

In keeping with much contemporary Jesus research, Crossan locates Jesus socially and economically in a first-century Palestinian context (Oakman, 1986; Horsley, 1987). Geography is also important. For Jesus was from Galilee, from Nazareth, 'a tiny hamlet whose population has been estimated at anything from twelve hundred to two hundred people' (Crossan, 1994, p. 26). Nazareth was only about three miles from Sepphoris, a large town (perhaps even a 'city'), and so Jesus would have had contact with the well-to-do and culturally sophisticated. But that, says Crossan, was not his own background. Being more of a rural Galilean, his primary work would have been 'among the farms and villages of Lower Galilee' (Crossan, 1991, p. 422). If he was a carpenter, as Mark 6:3 may suggest (the precise meaning of the Greek word *tekton* is disputed), then this implies he would be a maker of farming implements which he would sell around the region. And as such, socially he would have:

> belonged to the Artisan class, that group pushed into the dangerous space between Peasants and Degradeds or Expendables. (1994, p. 25)

In other words, although Jesus is socially and economically not in the lowest stratum of first-century Palestinian society, he is not far off it.

Jewish

In Crossan's view, Jesus began as a follower of John the Baptist. And John 'was an apocalyptic preacher announcing, in classical Jewish tradition, the imminent advent of an avenging God' (1994, p. 38). Crossan is not, however, convinced that Jesus remained consistent with John the Baptist's way of seeing things.

> The major question is not whether Jesus began as an apocalyptic believer but whether he continued as such and whether, when he began his own mission, he did so by picking up the fallen banner of the Baptist. (1994, p. 46)

Matthew 11:7b–9 (paralleled in Luke 7:24b–26 and *Thomas* 78) suggests that Jesus is quite different from John. This tradition is hardly likely to have been invented by early Christians, who seem to have been inclined to develop the eschatological interpretation of Jesus. Equally, the fact that it has not been suppressed or removed is a point in favour of its authenticity. Crossan notes that Jesus' form of Judaism seems to have conflicted with the apocalyptic strand. He is much closer to the Jewish wisdom tradition. Whatever may have been the cause of this 'conversion' of Jesus (possibly the death of John the Baptist), the result was that Jesus primarily focused on the here and now.

> An alternative to the future or apocalyptic Kingdom is the present or sapiential vision. The term *sapiential* underlines the necessity of wisdom – *sapientia* in Latin – for discerning how, here and now in this world, one can live so that God's power, rule, and dominion are evidently present to all observers... It is a style of life for now rather

than a hope of life for the future. (1994, p. 56)

It is, however, important to note that Crossan claims to be able to retain an 'eschatological' element to his interpretation of the kingdom of God, even though he rejects the apocalyptic strand. By 'eschatological' Crossan means 'world-negating'. And this, he says, is very much part of his wisdom-oriented reading of Jesus. Jesus is no less suspicious of the world of which he is a part, even though he differs from John the Baptist's apocalypticism.

Cynic

The world-negating aspect of Jesus' teaching and practice relates directly to the third component in Crossan's description of Jesus as a 'peasant Jewish Cynic'. 'Cynicism' is a Greek philosophical movement which goes back to the fourth century BCE. The extent to which it was a widespread movement throughout the Mediterranean world is disputed in New Testament studies today. However, there are undoubtedly features of Jesus' practice which relate to Cynic-like practices, even if it is difficult to demonstrate explicitly that Jesus was linked to Cynicism.

The most striking similarity between Jesus, his followers and the Cynics relates to what they wear. Crossan thinks that Luke 10:4 (Q) is earlier than Mark 6:8–9, and sees the command not to wear sandals as the original version. Thus Jesus' followers would have looked like wandering Cynics. But what about the carrying of possessions? Here there are apparent differences. Cynics were to carry a wallet, a staff and a cloak with them at all times, even if the cloak was to be old and torn. Jesus' followers were told to take no bread or bag or money, though they were permitted a staff to aid walking. Why the difference? Crossan's explanation is simple:

> They are not urban like the Cynics, preaching at street corner and market place. They are rural, on a house mission to rebuild peasant society from the grass roots upward... they could not and should not dress to declare itinerant self-sufficiency but rather communal dependency. (1994, pp. 118–19)

Jesus therefore started a Cynic-like movement, possibly as a result of his own contacts with Cynics in Sepphoris (which was, after all, a 'Greco-Roman city'). But he modified their practice, given his own background as a rural Galilean from the artisan class. But what was Cynicism about? In practice (which is where Crossan wants to put the emphasis), it meant overturning social conventions and resisting the normal assumptions of civilized society. Jesus was concerned to question and challenge the way in which Greco-Roman society took shape in first-century Palestine.

Thus he embarked on an itinerant ministry which focused on the rural poor, his outlook profoundly influenced by peasantry, Judaism and Cynicism. But what form did this mission take? Crossan's exposition of Jesus' life and teaching focuses, not surprisingly, on the socially subversive elements recorded in the Gospels. This does not simply mean Jesus' eating-habits, shocking though they were ('All who saw it began to grumble and said, "He has gone to be the guest of one who is a sinner"', Luke 19:7). It also relates to Jesus' healing and exorcistic activity. To modern readers, this aspect of Jesus' ministry sets him apart from all others and has often been used to 'prove' his messiahship or divinity. But Crossan suggests that a close reading of the Gospels shows that the focus is actually on social inclusion. Jesus does not perform healings and exorcisms in order to confer some special status on the sick (or himself). He restores them, both individually and socially. His aim was to reintegrate those who have been ostracized by society, such as lepers, the possessed, the haemorrhaged woman.

Crossan has no qualms, then, about claiming that 'the historical Jesus had both an ideal vision and a social program' (1991, p. 349). Unlike the Weiss-Schweitzer-Sanders approach, Crossan's Jesus is focused on the here and now. There is a kingdom to be preached and enacted, but it is a present, sapiential kingdom and is not simply to be awaited. And God is certainly not to be coerced or petitioned, in order to bring it about. In keeping with the Jewish wisdom tradition of which Jesus is a part, loyal to his economic and social background, and influenced by the ascetics he may have come across who questioned the administrative and political heavy-handedness of the Roman authorities, Jesus set about a practical programme of transforming Galilean society by the personal influence of a small movement of people. Here, says Crossan, is the heart of the original Jesus movement:

> a shared egalitarianism of spiritual and material resources. I emphasize this as strongly as possible, and I insist that its materiality and spirituality, its facticity and symbolism cannot be separated. The mission we are talking about is not, like Paul's, a dramatic thrust along major trade routes to urban centers hundreds of miles apart. Yet it concerns the longest journey in the Greco-Roman world, maybe in any world, the step across the threshold of a peasant stranger's home. (1991, p. 341)

More Cynics?

We have given a lot of space to Crossan's work because it is very influential in New Testament study at present. It would be wrong, though, to think that Crossan is alone in challenging the view of Jesus as primarily an eschatological prophet, who looked to an imminently future kingdom of God. Nor would it be right to claim that this recent, predominantly North American way of interpreting Jesus is completely new, though the connection with Cynicism and the use of the *Gospel of Thomas* is distinctive. We must now look at other scholars who take a similar approach to Crossan, and at some precursors of the emphases of this second major strand of Jesus-interpretation.

Marcus Borg is an especially interesting interpreter of Jesus because at the same time as contributing major research into the Jesus of history (Borg, 1984, 1987, 1994a), he has also made several attempts, in a way that many Jesus scholars do not, to draw out the implications of his work for practical everyday Christian faith (Borg, 1994b, 1997; Borg and Wright, 1998). Borg should be considered alongside Crossan simply because he has so strenuously resisted the image of Jesus as an eschatological figure. At the same time as offering an understanding of the social and political background of Jesus (1984), and a reading of Jesus as 'sage' ('teacher of wisdom') and 'revitalization movement founder' (1987, pp. 97–149), his picture of Jesus adds a number of features to those gleaned from Crossan.

First, Borg addresses what for long has been considered a 'no-go zone' in modern biblical scholarship: Jesus' spiritual experience. Without delving too deeply into Jesus' inner life (not as deep as John Miller in his 1997 work *Jesus at Thirty*), Borg is nevertheless prepared to consider the kind of spiritual experience which must have been known by one who did the things that Jesus did. Accepting the strangeness of the first-century world which we are seeking to interpret, Borg stitches together a number of features of the Gospel accounts of Jesus which cannot be sidestepped: visions, his practice of prayer and the authoritative impact his person seemed to have on others.

A second feature is that Borg retains a prominent place for Jesus' role and function as a prophet, even though he offers a non-eschatological interpretation of Jesus. This raises the question as to what kind of prophet Jesus was, if not the kind suggested by the Weiss-Schweitzer-Sanders tradition. Borg's understanding links Jesus directly with the classical prophets of Israel and their roles as God's messengers, operating out of 'the intensity of their experience of the Spirit' (1987, p. 150). The prophets, however, were quite clearly political, in the sense that they read the signs of the times; they weren't predicters of the future with a special hot-line to God. They followed, says Borg, a three-fold pattern of indictment, threat and call to change, accompanying their spoken message with symbolic actions.

Jesus followed a similar pattern of ministry at a particular time of crisis in his people's history. Rather than connecting his reading of Jesus with the Weiss-Schweitzer-Sanders tradition, however, Borg prefers to see Jesus' own prophetic convictions in terms of 'the threat of historical catastrophe for his society' (1987, p. 157). It is wrong, then, to make Jesus too other-worldly. And this, for Borg, seems to be the essential error behind the eschatological reading of Jesus. It was certainly present in Schweitzer's interpretation of Jesus. Whether it was equally true of Weiss and Sanders is not easy to judge. Borg is stressing more than either of those scholars that the sense of urgency in Jesus' mission and ministry is more concerned with social, economic and political factors than with the expectation of an other-worldly kingdom. Furthermore, he wants to emphasize these necessary elements, without claiming that Jesus' mission and ministry is *reducible* to them. In other words, social, economic and political factors do not explain away Jesus' ministry, as if his relationship with God and his own inner life somehow did not count. Borg is at pains to see how a spiritual life interweaves with such elements. Jesus' prophetic role leads him to advocate 'the politics of compassion' in place of 'the politics of holiness', and this inevitably leads him to offer a fundamental challenge to Judaism, *but always from within.*

Wright's interpretation of Jesus has many points of contact with Borg's. As we saw in the previous chapter, Wright, too, wants to point out the concrete aspects of the words and actions of Jesus. He, too, is sceptical of readings of Jesus which understand the kingdom of God in some other-worldly sense. On the contrary, says Wright, even apocalyptic visions are essentially about this-worldly events. His position is clearly stated:

> there is no justification for seeing 'apocalyptic' as necessarily speaking of the 'end of the world' in a literally cosmic sense... we must read most apocalyptic literature, both Jewish and Christian, as a complex metaphor-system which invests space-time reality with its full, that is, its theological, significance. (1992, pp. 298–9)

But ultimately Wright feels unable to accept Borg's argument for a non-eschatological Jesus. For even though Wright has no desire to push the aims and actions of Jesus beyond this world, nevertheless, his reading of Jesus in the Gospels leads him to conclude that Jesus himself thought that, in him, the end had come. Whether through collusion with the ruling powers (Sadducees) or armed resistance (Zealots),

Jesus was convinced that Israel must return to God or face the consequences. He thus has much in common with Sanders' 'Jewish restoration theology', even though there are also elements in common with the more diverse group being considered here. All of this shows just how slippery such terms as 'kingdom', 'eschatology' and 'apocalyptic' can be, as is particularly apparent when we consider the earlier work of William Wrede and C.H. Dodd.

Wrede and Dodd

Glance at most textbook treatments of Wrede and you can be sure that the word 'radical' will not be far away. If German New Testament scholarship at the end of the nineteenth century was known to be radical, then Wrede was certainly one of the reasons for this. With hindsight, his questions, though searching, were not that extreme. It was more the novelty of his willingness to pose them and to take some challenging lines of thought to their logical conclusion, which proved most shocking. For our purposes, we need to note two of his insights. The first concerns the framework of Mark's Gospel. The earliest testimony to Mark (Papias) says that, 'Mark, who had been Peter's interpreter, wrote down carefully, but not in order, all that he remembered' (see Appendix). This admission of inaccuracy had not been of great concern to the church since Luke claims to have written 'an orderly account' and Matthew became the church Gospel. But as Mark was increasingly being recognized as the earliest Gospel and as providing the narrative framework for Matthew and Luke, this conclusion became crucial. If Mark is not in order then neither are Matthew and Luke, and so it becomes doubtful if a 'life of Jesus' (in the sense of a biography) can be written.

Wrede's second insight was the idea of the 'messianic secret'. Wrede was puzzled by the fact that the Gospel writers portray Jesus telling his disciples and those who are healed to keep his identity secret, while performing miracles that led to huge acclamation. Wrede's conclusion is simple: Jesus did not ask people to keep quiet. The command to silence is a fictional element in the narrative, introduced by Mark (or those before him) as a sort of apology for the disciples' failure to recognize at the time what the church later proclaimed about Jesus' identity. According to Wrede, Jesus never claimed to be the Messiah and did not think of himself thus. It should be noted that this does not automatically nullify the church's teaching. It is clear from the New Testament that the resurrection of Jesus caused a radical re-evaluation of his earthly life. Perhaps 'messiahship' was kept from him, just as Mark admits that Jesus did not know when the 'Son of Man' would come (13:32). But the idea that Jesus did not know that he was the Messiah is more disturbing.

Wrede's contribution to Gospel research, and its relevance to this chapter's subject-matter, should now be clear. The possibility of a non-messianic Jesus, recovered by a Christian scholar, opens up a new range of options for Christian interpretations of the Gospels. No longer need one conclude, even as a Christian, that the Gospels must lead one to a Jesus who knew himself to be the Messiah and claimed himself to be such. Perhaps Jesus was so different from current expectations that the term 'messiah' was inappropriate. After all, many of the messianic expectations (conversion of the Gentiles, universal peace, new heaven and earth) had clearly not happened. In what sense would Jesus have thought himself to be the Messiah when many of the messianic expectations remained unfulfilled?

The possibility of a non-eschatological Jesus was given further support by the British scholar C.H. Dodd three decades later. In a number of publications, beginning with *The Parables of the Kingdom* in 1935, Dodd espoused the view that Jesus promoted a 'realized eschatology': the kingdom is not simply a future hope but was present in Jesus. Such passages as Matthew 11:2–11; 12:28 (= Luke 11:20); Mark 1:14–15; Luke 7:18–30; 10:9–11,23–4 (= Matt 13:16–17), Luke 11:31–2 (= Matt 12:41–2) and Luke 16:16 are adduced to determine a 'fixed point' from which an understanding of Jesus' teaching on the kingdom should begin. Realized eschatology is about 'the impact upon this world of the "powers of the world to come" in a series of events, unprecedented and unrepeatable, now in actual process' (Dodd, 1961, p. 41). It thus encapsulated a persuasive argument for attending to the present, this-worldly dimension of Jesus' ministry.

For Dodd, however, eschatology also remained firmly in the picture. He knew he could not sidestep eschatology, it being, for him, the cradle within which Christianity was born, and without reference to which early Christian preaching cannot be understood. Nor did he exclude the possibility that Jesus himself offered predictions about the future. But he suggested that early Christians had evidently stressed the eschatological context and content of Jesus' mission in a particular way, adding some rather unhelpful apocalyptic trimmings in the process. Interpreters of the Gospels therefore need carefully to pick up the more insightful readings of eschatology which, though they are themselves a form of theological interpretation, nevertheless more accurately get to the heart of what Jesus was about.

Dodd is, therefore, very positive about the fourth Gospel. He draws the reader's attention to it on two fronts. First, he asks whether there may be elements within it that provide independent historical tradition about Jesus (Dodd, 1963). Secondly, he suggests that passages such as John 5:25–9 are of the profoundest significance for the way that early Christianity reworked eschatology. For Dodd, such interpretations are more true to Jesus' intent than the apocalyptic speculations which were also part of Christianity's early history. With Jesus the end had indeed come, but not in the way that customary understandings of 'the end' might have expected.

At this point we have come full circle. The eschatological emphasis of the previous chapter has been well and truly undercut. Dodd is shaking hands with Crossan. And even though the Crossan-Borg-Wrede-Dodd approach is in no way as neat as the interpretation of Jesus as an eschatological prophet, nevertheless we have found enough points of contact to suggest that it is an identifiable tradition. Let us summarize some of its main points:

- The focus is upon Jesus' relationship to this world. His ministry and mission, summed up in words and actions about the kingdom of God, are primarily about the present.
- The sources are ambiguous as to whether Jesus actually claimed to be the Messiah. This might be because he did not think of himself in these terms, even if it was very significant for the early church.
- Radical suspicion of the Gospels is therefore quite appropriate, alongside a proper respect, given the many things which are going on in them (including the incorporation of elements which might not have happened exactly as the text says).
- All four Gospels are a blend of history and theology and can be used in determining who Jesus was. Mark's suffering Jesus may be closer to the 'historical Jesus' or may result from Mark's own particular emphases. Each incident and saying must be considered on its own merits.
- The more we attend to Jesus' relation to his own present world, the more we have to deal with the social, economic and political aspects of his world.
- Jesus' Jewishness is crucial for understanding him, as is the way in which he evidently undermined it from within, together with challenging the Greco-Roman cultural customs of his time.

One further observation should conclude this section. Although it is a generalization to say that Chapter 7 relates more to the Jesus of Matthew and Mark, and this chapter to Luke and John, nevertheless it is worth noting. It is surely not coincidental that the Jesus Seminar, of which two of the scholars considered in this chapter are members (Crossan and Borg), should have concluded that there is proportionately more historically reliable material in Luke's Gospel than in the other Gospels. Luke's Gospel emphasizes Jesus' crossing of customary social boundaries through his contact with children, women, government officials, Roman soldiers, Gentiles and the demon-possessed. Though by no means exclusive to Luke, these features are drawn out more in his Gospel. Nor can it be coincidental that John's Gospel is effectively reinstated in the quest for the historical Jesus by those who argue that he was a non-eschatological figure.

There may, of course, be all sorts of factors at work here, not merely to do with the supposedly disinterested quest for the Jesus of history. In Chapter 10 we shall take up the material from our opening chapter and press the question as to what those factors might be.

A provisional assessment

What are we to make of this loose affiliation of supporters of the non-eschatological Jesus? Inevitably, the material from the previous chapter could be seen as counter-evidence against this chapter's thinking. There seems to be so much eschatological urgency in the synoptic Gospels to modify the material which presents Jesus as primarily interested in social subversion. And isn't this form of the 'this-wordly' Jesus just a little too modern (even postmodern)? Have Dodd and Crossan, in their own different ways, tried to turn Jesus into a figure who speaks to the present age as a radical cultural critic? Does not Borg want to have his cake and eat it, trying to confine all aspects of Jesus into a single interpretation which ultimately bursts the bounds of possibility? And doesn't the line of thinking deriving from Wrede, which has proved so influential throughout the twentieth century, simply run out of steam when faced with the question: why, then, does Christianity exist?

The readiness with which Crossan and others ascribe an early date to the *Gospel of Thomas* (or at least the sayings preserved within it) cannot go unchallenged. This does not relate, of course, to the dating of manuscripts, as only scraps of text for any of the Gospels come from the late first century; the first full available texts date from much later. However, the reliability of *Thomas* as a historical record is questionable. It may contain some early forms of parables and sayings but its overall picture of Jesus is suspect. Consider, for example, his attitude to women, which differs markedly from the synoptics:

> Simon Peter said to them, 'Let Mary leave us, because women are not worthy of life.' Jesus said, 'Look, I shall lead her so that I will make her male in order that she also may become a living spirit, resembling you males. For every woman who makes herself male will enter the kingdom of heaven.' (*Thomas* 114)

It is one thing to include *Thomas* in the available data. It is another to promote it above the canonical Gospels. Furthermore, the alliance between *Thomas* and Q depends not only on the hypothesis that Q was an actual document but also on a theory about its composition. Q, as reconstructed, contains both wisdom and eschatological sayings, and does not in itself help Crossan's cause. It is only the theory that the eschatological sayings are a later addition that supports his case. But is this simply saying that when the eschatological sayings are removed from the Gospels, we are left with a non-eschatological Jesus?

A second critical point concerns the location of the wisdom-oriented Jesus within first-century Judaism. Some object to Crossan's Jesus on the grounds that not only is he not Jewish enough, he is also akin to some of the anti-Semitic pictures of Jesus which were offered in the first half of the twentieth century. But such criticisms are misplaced. Crossan's point is that you have to be clear into which part of Judaism Jesus fits best. In that respect he is no different from the scholars considered in the previous chapter. But the lack of plausibility of Crossan's Jesus *at all points*, in particular his tendency to over-emphasize wisdom, is perhaps explained by Borg's need to do greater justice to the prophetic element in the Gospel tradition. One might have expected much wider evidence of support for a 'sapiential kingdom' in first-century Judaism than appears to be the case. Although Dodd subverts readings of Jesus which emphasize the future aspect of the kingdom of God, he also acknowledges that eschatology *is* the matrix of early Christianity. In other words, more wrestling with the Gospel materials is required than Crossan's account implies. It is not surprising, in the development of New Testament study in the twentieth century, that even while Dodd's corrective of Schweitzer was favourably received, it resulted in an understanding of the kingdom of God as both present *and* future (Chilton, 1984, pp. 1–26).

Thirdly, what Wrede perceived (that early Christian theology profoundly affected the Gospels' description of Jesus), is surely true of contemporary scholars too. It happens with most scholars, of course, but with Dodd and perhaps also with Borg, insights from Christian theology may well be influencing their reading of the historical evidence. Both these scholars are interested in the relationship between the historical Jesus and the development and present content of Christian theology. This does not immediately make the history 'wrong', nor is the practice illegitimate. We shall, in the final chapter, draw out more fully how facts and interpretation interweave. But a tendency to stress the present, this-worldly character of the message and ministry of Jesus is more likely to be evident when someone is looking specifically for the present significance of Jesus. And this will be significant for Christian faith. It highlights the extent to which tackling 'Jesus and the Gospels' is never just a matter of trying to locate the Jesus of history. It emphasizes, too, how hard it is to find the 'Jesus of history' at all.

Two traditions are not enough

The work of Wright has featured in both this and the previous chapter. This itself provides evidence that a 'two-track' approach to understanding Jesus within the Gospels is ultimately not enough. It is useful, but problematic. There are always scholars who do not fit into either track, either because they seem to be in, or outside, both. Wright himself has seen this, noting that Dodd's work is not easy to place (though even Wright still speaks of two roads: a Schweitzer Street and a Wrede Highway, and he places himself on the former). We have placed him here, while respecting that he wants to be located more with scholars in the previous chapter.

The neatness of such a structure belies the complexity of what the Gospels actually present to us. A structure erected largely on historical grounds will not do justice to what the Gospels are, and what they are trying to do. Historical research should rightly get us looking critically at the Gospels. But it is unable to offer the last word on what the Evangelists were up to, and what their texts can still achieve in the present. In the next chapter, we shall explore other interpretations of Jesus which fit even less neatly into these two basic categories, before concluding our study with some reflections on all that is involved when readers of the Gospels try to interpret the multi-faceted figure of Jesus.

9

Jesus, Gospels and different interests

As we have already noted, not all studies of Jesus fit neatly into the two main categories that we have been considering. This is true even if our goal is purely historical, for there are always going to be many ways of viewing the evidence. And this is even more true if we remember what was said in the first chapter concerning the nature of the Gospels. They are not aiming simply to transmit historical data. They are aiming to transmit a picture of Jesus that will evoke belief and will stir readers and hearers to particular actions. In this chapter, therefore, we will look at other writings about Jesus which emphasize the function of the Gospel stories.

Jesus as political liberator

The study of Jesus in the social, economic and political context of first-century Palestine does not necessarily turn Jesus himself into an explicitly political figure. Politics and religion are usually said to have been more closely intertwined in the first century than they often are today. Jesus was undoubtedly a political figure, simply because of the impact of his religious views and actions. But there is clearly a difference between Jesus and Pilate or between Jesus and Judas of Galilee (often called 'the founder of the Zealots'), and even between Jesus and Judas Iscariot, whatever the precise reasons for Judas' betrayal. Of the scholars we examined in the last chapter, Crossan, while declaring that Jesus had a 'social program', holds back from saying that Jesus was a politician, even if an itinerant Cynic with an ideal vision and a social programme was as close to being a politician as a rural peasant in Galilee ever could be. Borg pressed the political implications of Jesus' words and actions most strongly. But he did not push his conclusions as far as Jon Sobrino.

Jon Sobrino is a Spanish Roman Catholic theologian who has spent most of his life working in El Salvador. He is one of the leading exponents of liberation theology, a way of doing theology which became prominent in Latin America in the 1960s and 1970s. This challenged the seemingly abstract forms of theological reflection undertaken in Europe and North America by demanding that more attention be paid to the situations in which most people in the world actually lived. In the case of Latin America, and in Sobrino's own context in El Salvador, this meant trying to make sense of the Christian faith in the face of poverty and political violence. Sobrino's interest in the figure of Jesus is thus always historical for he is concerned to build into his thinking historically accurate details of Jesus' life and ministry. Sobrino is, however, equally keen to be open about his own context.

Sobrino's most influential book, *Christology at the Crossroads*, first published in English in 1978 (written in Spanish in 1976), is not only about the Gospels, or about Jesus as a historical figure. As a book about Christology, it discusses the way in which the figure of Jesus has become 'the Christ of faith'; it also discusses the history of Christological doctrines, and the understanding of Christ in the Ignatian Exercises (Sobrino is a Jesuit). There are also chapters about the resurrection of Jesus, which go well beyond what is warranted by the Gospel accounts alone. But even though it is explicitly about Christology, Sobrino connects it directly with 'the historical Jesus'.

In four historically focused chapters, Sobrino draws attention to four crucial features of the life of Jesus of Nazareth on which his theological reflection centres: the kingdom of God, Jesus' own faith, Jesus' attitude to prayer, and the death of Jesus. In each case, Sobrino presents what he deems to be the sure findings of historical-critical study of the Gospels, on the basis of which an extensive study in Christology can be built. He begins his third chapter, for example, by claiming: 'The most certain historical datum about Jesus' life is that the concept which dominated his preaching, the reality which gave meaningfulness to all his activity, was "the kingdom of God"... in historical terms we can only come to know the historical Jesus in and through the notion of God's kingdom' (Sobrino, 1978, p. 41). Few would dispute this. But what is striking is the extent to which Sobrino develops a political understanding of the kingdom of God. The kingdom is 'a restructuring of the visible, tangible relationships existing between human beings' (1978, p. 44). It entails overcoming a negative situation. Only thus understood can the kingdom be seen as liberation. In order to understand Jesus in the Gospels, then, we must pay special attention to the way in which the Gospel writers 'place Jesus in the midst of situations embodying divisiveness and oppression, where the good news and salvation can only be understood as being in total discontinuity with them' (1978, p. 47). Such situations include Jesus' relationships with leprosy sufferers,

Samaritans and other non-Jews, women and the demon-possessed. Sobrino also emphasizes that Jesus' expressions of opposition (e.g. Matt 23:13–39) are nearly always collective, that is, against groups. And they are always to do with the abuse of power.

Sobrino's attention to Jesus' own faith and his life of prayer are especially interesting. Sobrino's concern is always to examine Jesus' practice in very concrete terms. He sees two distinct phases in Jesus' life, with Mark 8 (Matt 13; Luke 8; John 6) as the turning point. In the first phase, Jesus lived as a good Jew in Galilee. But in the second, he moved around more, accepting that his earlier practice had been something of a failure and that more concerted action was needed. Sobrino thus claims to discern 'some rupture in his [i.e. Jesus'] inner consciousness and his outer activity, suggesting a rupture in his faith' (Sobrino, 1978, p. 94).

There is not space here to examine how Sobrino develops his reflections on the death of Jesus into a bold statement of the centrality of the cross for Christian faith and theology. But we must consider his attention to the death of Jesus in relation to his reading of the Gospels. For Sobrino, the death of Jesus is to be understood as the inevitable consequence of the second half of Jesus' life. Crucifixion and resurrection belong inextricably together, as indeed they are found in the Gospel traditions, and only make sense when seen in relation to the concrete, 'kingdom-of-God'-oriented activity of Jesus.

Sobrino's understanding of Jesus and the Gospels is difficult to assess. Its urgency and practical intent are obvious. He presents Jesus to elicit a response, not so that his readers merely accept his findings as an interesting academic argument before moving on to another book. Ultimately, his Jesus was a religious reformer, through whose death his followers' perceptions of God changed irrevocably. In his own views and spirituality, Jesus was not all that novel. He radicalized the Judaism of which he was a part. But in so doing, more became evident about the God he called 'Father'. It was God, the Father of Jesus, who acted in and beyond Jesus' life in a decisive way.

To put this picture together, Sobrino effectively cuts across the findings of scholars mentioned in our two previous chapters. He shares the concrete concern of Crossan, mixed with urgency created by an apocalyptic framework for understanding the kingdom of God. Throughout, he has historical confidence in what the Gospels (even John) say, though he acknowledges the Evangelists' own theological interests. There are even points where it is clear that Sobrino assumes that the Gospels' chronological account of Jesus' life is essentially historical. This is, after all, implicit within his attempt to speak of phases of Jesus' life.

Sobrino thus mixes a clear attention to the Jesus of history with a declared intention to be theological in a practical way. This makes his Jesus hard to evaluate on the same terms as most of the work we examined in Chapters 7 and 8. His conclusions are, however, crucial because they pose the question: what are we meant to do, having heard or read the Gospels? Sobrino reminds all readers that seeking to understand the Gospels is not just a matter of extracting data about the Jesus of history from them. Nor is it even about getting the right 'ideas' about Jesus, even in an orthodox theological sense. It is about following their central character.

Jesus and his movement: a feminist portrait

From Sobrino we turn to the feminist theologian and historian of early Christianity, Elisabeth Schüssler Fiorenza. Within her 'feminist theological reconstruction of Christian origins' (*In Memory of Her*, 1983), Fiorenza includes an important exposition not just of Jesus, but of the movement that gathered round him. Her account is based on a telling critique of 'androcentric' ways of thinking (approaches which always prioritize men's actions). These ways of thinking also tend to be rather individualistic. So Fiorenza re-reads the Gospels, in search of a Jesus who makes the best sense of the *basileia* (androcentrically called a 'kingdom'), that corporate entity around which his whole activity seemed to revolve.

Fiorenza's conclusions seem, at different points, very close to those of Crossan and Sobrino. She does, however, make a major contribution to the task of understanding Jesus which takes us beyond those we have considered so far. Fiorenza stresses that the central concept of Jesus' preaching and practice, the *basileia*, is a social concept. Therefore, it is a mistake for interpreters of Jesus to focus too closely on the individual figure of Jesus, in isolation from those around him. The *basileia* message is clearly directed towards the destitute, the sick and the crippled, the tax-collectors, the sinners and the prostitutes. Out of Jesus' socially subversive activity, a community of people results which enables people who had been ostracized to be 're-connected' socially. This is nothing other than a 'discipleship of equals', where customary social divisions no longer matter. This activity, as far as Jesus was concerned, was a clear sign that the end *had* come (Luke 10:18). Jesus had parted company with John the Baptist (Luke 17:21 challenges Matthew 3:10). It is not just in Jesus' own ministry, but in the movement which begins with that ministry, that the *basileia* is present.

What kind of images are best used for this? 'It is the festive table-sharing at a wedding feast' (1983, p. 119), rather than the religiosity of a holy man, that best describes the movement. Indeed, the contrast between the eating habits of John and Jesus was a point of public discussion (Mark 2:18). The *basileia* was for all, not merely a select few. Matthew 22:1–14 and Mark 10:31 confirm the subversive content of Jesus' preaching and practice. Fiorenza acknowledges that it is important to locate the earliest layers of the Gospel traditions, and she therefore finds in some Marcan material and in the material common to Matthew and Luke (Q) the most historically reliable data about Jesus. In her view, 'the oldest traditions elaborate concretely Jesus' reply to John that "the poor have good news preached to them"' (1983, p. 122).

Because of her feminist insights, Fiorenza is aware that historical work is always ideologically informed. In other words, we can and must try, as historians, to do our best to see 'what actually happened'. But as we cannot avoid making assumptions as we try to tease out 'what actually happened', we must actually use them to help us in our task. And ultimately, as interpreters of the Gospels, we should not be content with determining 'what actually happened'. We shall also want to know how the results of our enquiries enable us to believe in and think about God, and what we should do as a consequence. By combining the search for the earliest evidence with the awareness of what we, as readers, bring and do when we read texts, Fiorenza reaches a telling conclusion:

> While the earliest Jesus traditions eschew any understanding of the ministry and death of Jesus in cultic terms as atonement for sins, it was precisely this interpretation which soon took root in some segments of the early Christian movement. Yet such an interpretation of Jesus' death as atonement for sins is much later than is generally assumed in New Testament scholarship. The notion of atoning sacrifice does not express the Jesus movement's understanding and experience of God but is a later interpretation of the violent death of Jesus in cultic terms. (1983, p. 130)

Fiorenza is here making a historical judgement which cuts through the New Testament material. By being informed by feminist insights, however, her search for the earliest material has led her to re-read the early history of Christianity. Fiorenza's reading may seem to add little to what we have touched on already. Yet the profundity of her critique of so much Jesus research (still more evident in Fiorenza, 1995, pp. 73–88) and her insight that we should look at the movement around Jesus and not just at an isolated male individual, make her an important scholar to consider. In stressing the communal above the individual, feminist scholarship invites interpreters of Jesus to consider that the

Gospels and their central character may be best received by communities of followers rather than individual readers. Ultimately, then, Fiorenza's work raises the question of which communities (including churches) we, as Gospel readers, are located within when we try to interpret Jesus.

The combination of ideological awareness with the search for the earliest layers in the Gospels creates a tension in Fiorenza's work. For at the same time as stressing (rightly) the extent to which all historical studies reflect the ideologies and contexts of those who offer them, and criticizing scholars who overlook such factors, she is nevertheless holding up the Jesus of the earliest strata as the most important in her own reading. But we have already seen (in Chapter 7) that the 'oldest is best' argument should not necessarily always win the day. Simply because you uncover an early layer does not necessarily mean you have offered the most accurate reading of Jesus. Fiorenza's emphasis on other factors which are inevitably entailed in reading the Gospels is, however, a point to which we shall need to return.

Jesus as spiritual and ethical example

The third contemporary portrait is in one sense not Christian. That is to say, it would not be regarded as sufficient by most Christians (it does not say enough about Jesus as the Christ, the redeemer sent by God). Nevertheless, there are many people who are influenced by it, both consciously and unconsciously. They 'believe' in the sermon on the mount or the good Samaritan or the command to love one's neighbour as oneself. This type of reading is less concerned about historical scholarship as such. Whether Jesus was exactly as the Gospels present him is not of great importance. It is, in practice, more interested in how the Gospels as texts inspire people to ethical action or spiritual insight, even if it is always assumed that Jesus the historical figure had inspired their writing. After all, Jesus told his hearers to 'go and do likewise' (Luke 10:37; Matt 7:24), not 'use my words to construct a doctrinal system'.

Our first example is taken from the German novelist Heinrich Böll (1978). As with many such volumes which ask famous people to choose meaningful texts from the Bible, Böll has selected his favourite passages. But this is no off-the-cuff selection. The title of the chapter in which Böll has drawn this material together refers to 'True Righteousness'. Thus he 'connects' primarily with the ethical imperatives contained in the words, actions and stories of Jesus. His main passages are:

Matt 5:1–12   The beatitudes
Matt 5:13–16   The salt of the earth and the light of the world
Matt 18:23–35   The parable of the unmerciful believer
Matt 25:14–30   The parable of the entrusted money
Mark 7:24–30   The Syrophoenician woman's request
Luke 7:36–50   Jesus' encounter with the sinful woman
Luke 8:1–3   Women among the followers of Jesus
Luke 15:11–32   The parable of the lost son
Luke 16:1–8   The parable of the clever manager
Luke 16:9–13   The correct use of wealth
John 4:7–18   Conversation with a Samaritan woman
John 7:53 – 8:11   Jesus and the adulteress

Böll's selection focuses upon the impact and continuing significance of the ethical teaching of Jesus. These cut across the Gospels, and reflect Böll's concern to work out, in the present, how human beings are to act. This is not all that Böll says about Jesus. We are simply using his selection of material here as an example of what goes on when people actually use the Gospels. An image of Jesus (moral teacher and exemplar) is 'constructed' by the reader, in relation to their own concerns.

A second example comes from the introduction to Mark's Gospel by the musician Nick Cave in the *pocket canons* series. Cave writes:

> *The Gospel According to Mark* has continued to inform my life as the root source of my spirituality, my religiousness. The Christ that the Church offers us, the bloodless, placid 'Saviour' – the man smiling benignly at a group of children, or calmly, serenely hanging from the cross – denies Christ His potent, creative sorrow or His boiling anger that confronts us so forcefully in *Mark*. Thus the Church denies Christ His humanity, offering up a figure that we can perhaps 'praise', but never relate to. The essential humanness of *Mark's* Christ provides us with a blueprint for our own lives, so that we have something that we can aspire to, rather than revere, that can lift us free of the mundanity of our existences, rather than affirming the notion that we are lowly and unworthy. Merely to praise Christ in His Perfectness, keeps us on our knees, with our heads pitifully bent. Clearly, this is not what Christ had in mind. Christ came as a liberator. Christ understood that we as humans were for ever held to the ground by the pull of gravity – our ordinariness, our mediocrity – and it was through His example that He gave our imaginations the freedom to rise and to fly. In short, to be Christ-like. (Cave, 1998, pp. xi–xii)

The word 'blueprint', and the fact that Cave was and is looking for an example to follow, shows how the Jesus of Mark functions for him.

Unlike Böll, who drew his ethical insights from Jesus by ranging across the canonical Gospels, Cave focuses on the Jesus of Mark (not Matthew, Luke, John or Thomas). The urgency of the narrative, the humanness of the Jesus portrayed, both prove compelling for him.

Two things are worth noting here. First, Cave clearly believes that he has got hold of, or is close to, what Jesus of Nazareth himself was actually like ('Clearly, this is not what Christ had in mind. Christ came as a liberator'). It matters, then, what Jesus was like, even if historical enquiry has not been a reader's main concern. This leads to a second point: Cave is using Mark, in a way that many people (even in churches!) would support, to be critical of what the churches themselves have made of Jesus Christ. Cave wants Jesus to critique the church. In doing so, Cave observes something which has been long seen, but not often taken into account, that there is a conversation beginning already in the New Testament about who Jesus the Christ was and is. And perhaps even the New Testament accounts, let alone the interpretations of Jesus which have been offered in Christian history since, are not fully reconcilable with each other.

We have presented, then, just two examples of what happens when people inside and outside churches read the Gospels, and become influenced by the figure of Jesus. Clearly, this is what Christian believers do all the time, in their own devotional and spiritual life: they read the Gospels selectively, can 'relate' more easily to some parts than others, and are influenced by some aspects but not others. This is inevitable, but creates problems. Individual readers can dodge bits which are uncomfortable, and overlook aspects which don't connect with their experience. Even if they do not simply 'create Jesus in their own image', they can at least construct a Jesus for their own purposes. The practice, while inevitable, therefore invites us to consider what provisos might be needed.

The bulk of Chapters 7 and 8 of this book concentrated on one main way in which a check on possible readings of the Gospels can be made. If Jesus is being talked about, then it is essential that we do our best to find out what Jesus was actually like. That in itself then limits how much we are able to say. This 'quest of the historical Jesus' is, and will remain, a key component in the task of interpreting the Gospels. But because the Gospels themselves already offer their own interpretations of Jesus, we must look beyond the historical data. What the Evangelists themselves want us to hear and do about Jesus, is clearly not confined to logging historical data. That is why Cave's comments are especially interesting. They move beyond history, because Cave wants to see the figure of Jesus not just in a historical light, but also as a contemporary influence.

The 'canonical Jesus' as the Christ of faith

A final contemporary way of reading the Jesus of the Gospels starts at the opposite end from Cave. It acknowledges that some kind of harmony across the canonical Gospels must be possible. For Christian faith is belief in the presence and action of God in the one Jesus Christ. Across the whole New Testament canon, then, it must be possible to speak of 'the biblical Christ', or, as we are suggesting, 'the canonical Jesus'. Martin Kähler, towards the end of the nineteenth century, suggested that it was misguided to try and find 'the historical Jesus' by stripping away all theological interpretation from the Gospel accounts. The result would simply be a lot of non-theological Jesuses, which would a) get Jesus wrong; and b) deny the actual function of the New Testament to present a single Christ.

On this approach, then, a view of Jesus must be found which takes account of a faith perspective, yet which does not deny the differences between the Gospels. Such a view will have a harmonizing and unifying function and will therefore not be welcomed by all. However, historical readings also have a harmonizing, unifying function. They simply unify the material of the Gospels in a different way. One of the strengths of separating out the different Gospels and not reading them 'synoptically', is to let them have their own say, on their own terms. But the great strength of looking for a 'canonical Jesus' is that it permits the theological interpretations of Jesus, which the Evangelists begin to present, to play a significant role. This is not constructing a 'Christmas-card Christology' by laying the material from all the Gospels alongside each other, as if all were of equal value. There will still need to be judicious sifting of the material. Decisions will still need to be made as to which Evangelist seems to give us a more profound insight at particular points. But we are not now only speaking of historical accuracy. Nor are we simply looking for what fits neatly into later Christian doctrine (otherwise how could Bible and doctrine ever stand in their essential creative tension?). We are concerned, though, with theology. We want to let the Gospels speak about God, as they speak about Jesus (and this, in their different ways, is what they seem to want to do). This approach can look forward, as well as back, from the text of the Gospels. It can acknowledge that the Gospels stimulated a whole history of interpretation of Jesus within the Christian church. That history, doctrinal and credal, is relevant to how we read the Gospels themselves.

A 'canonical Jesus' would be compatible with any of the interpretations of Jesus offered so far. What would be different, though, would be the material which other accounts could not so easily take in. For example, an account of the Jesus of history would not usually include reference to the birth narratives of Matthew or Luke (Bockmuehl, 1994, p. 41). Such texts are usually examined for what they tell us about their writers (as in Chapters 3–4). Here, though, we can take up some of their material as insight into Jesus himself, even while acknowledging that it may be myth or legend as it stands. Thus one of the main points in Luke's account of the shepherds appears to be that Jesus Christ has come for the poor, the outsiders, who are not only among the primary witnesses to the lowly nature of the presence of God in the world, but also play an active part in spreading the message (Luke 2:17). This may not be strictly historical (in the sense that this may well never have happened). But it may be true theologically.

Other examples of stories of this kind, which may not be historical in the sense that they probably did not happen in the way described, include:

Jesus' presence in the temple as a boy (Luke 2:41–52)
The temptation narratives (Matt 4:1–11 = Luke 4:1–13)
Jesus preaching in the synagogue (Luke 4:16–21)
Jesus walking on water (Mark 6:45–52)
The transfiguration (Mark 9:2–8)
Jesus and the woman at the well (John 4:1–42)
The death and raising of Lazarus (John 11:1–44)
The resurrection appearances (Matt 28:1–20; Luke 24:1–49; John
     20–1)
The ascension (Luke 24:50–3)

To a greater or lesser degree, all these stories have proved difficult to support as 'definitely having happened' as they are reported. To remain content with such questioning about them, however, is to miss a crucial point: they are told by the Evangelists not simply to give us historical information. The interpreter of Jesus and the Gospels who is interested not *just* in history, and not *just* in the theology of the Evangelists, but also in the theological significance of these texts for today, must therefore wrestle with them. For much of this material will be part of anyone's attempt to offer a reading of the canonical Jesus.

This does not mean that such material can simply be adopted uncritically. What matters is that it is not the historians who decide whether this material is any use for theology. Nor does it mean that there are no grounds for preferring one Evangelist over another at significant points. In the same way that historians may gravitate towards one Evangelist rather than another as a more reliable guide in their quest for the historical Jesus, so a theological interpreter may feel that Matthew (or Mark, or Luke, or John) may have got Jesus theologically 'more right' than the rest. But good reasons for any preference will always need to be provided.

It is not, of course, only the texts above which are open to the charge of not having happened. The same kind of argument could be applied to many Gospel narratives. However, parable-telling, meals out with a wide range of people, and even healings and exorcisms, are simply more 'history-like' than most of the texts just listed. But with any material in the Gospels, it is perfectly possible to argue that it simply 'didn't happen like this'. Whether something did or did not happen in the way reported (if we could even know) is not itself sufficient reason for establishing that such a passage has little or no theological value. At root, the Gospels are about God. They are simply texts which tell the story of Jesus in order to speak about God, and, in theological perspective, that is how they are to be received and used.

On this basis, even John's more baffling material, including that which bears no relation to the other canonical Gospels (e.g. its prologue, the revelation discourses, the farewell prayer), is usable. Indeed, it is not surprising that such material has frequently been the controlling factor in the church's use of the Gospels. For John seems to be the high point of New Testament Christology. The question which has to be asked about John, bearing in mind that it has been used in a distinct way within Christian doctrine, is whether its material genuinely draws out the theological significance of what we find in the other Gospels. It is not a case of Matthew, Mark and Luke being historical, and John theological. They are all theological and all historical in different ways. But how much of any particular Gospel is included within a version of 'the canonical Jesus' will depend on whether one thinks, for example, that the synoptics should be read through John, or the Gospel of Luke used to control one's reading of the others. And that decision will be based on a wide range of factors.

Selectivity, then, will play a role in the construction of a 'canonical Jesus'. But here, it will be due in large part to theological influences. The moment someone is prepared to say, 'when I have to do with Jesus, I believe that I have to do with God', then they are expressing a theological interest. If they are Christians, then they will also be wanting to take account of how the Christian church has read the Gospels and built doctrine around them. If they are authorized preachers or ministers in any Christian church, they will, to some extent at least, be bound by those later interpretations. But even doctrine changes.

Summary

In this chapter we have looked at four further pictures of Jesus which relate directly to the Gospels. The first two, those of Sobrino and

Fiorenza, seem to be similar in kind to those considered in the previous two chapters. They are views of the Jesus of history as he was. Their respective authors, however, are quite explicit about other interests in their work which they know to be present. This does not of itself devalue what they have come up with. Indeed, it may merely make us a bit more suspicious of those who profess to have come up with a more neutral picture.

The third image, of which we gave two concrete examples, related Jesus directly to ethical conduct. One of the examples was a composite image based on material from across the four canonical Gospels. The other was focused on Mark. Uppermost here were Jesus' ethical teaching and a particular Evangelist's Gospel. Yet even here, it seemed to be important that the text related back to the person of Jesus 'as he was'.

In considering the fourth image, we acknowledged that Christian believers are quite explicitly seeking to offer a theological reading of Jesus. Aspects of the Gospels which may therefore not be of great interest to historians become significant.

Through this brief survey of a number of images of Jesus beyond the two main historically focused tracks we considered earlier, it has become clear that we must do much more with the Gospels than apply to them the methods of historical scholarship. If it was wrong to try to prevent subjecting the Gospels to historical critique (as the Christian church has sometimes sought to do), it is equally wrong to prevent the Gospels being read in a wide range of ways, so that their central character has a chance to be more fully understood. In this chapter we have seen some of the many interests at work when people read the Gospels. In the final chapter we will spell them out in more detail.

10

How Christology works: the Gospels in practice

It should be clear by now that the historical way is not the only way to read the Gospels. It is entirely appropriate to apply the methods of historical criticism to the Gospels to discover, as far as possible, the historical person who gave rise to these accounts. But the Gospels are also narratives, intended to evoke in the reader certain images of Jesus, which the writers believed to be true. Redaction criticism and the more recent literary approaches to the Gospels have all tried to clarify what these images are and why the author emphasized them. However, even with the help of such studies, not everyone will see the same images of Jesus when they read the Gospels. What one sees is influenced by one's own concerns, background and social location among other things. It is the purpose of this final chapter to try to articulate these factors and to show how they affect our reading of the Gospels and the search for the historical figure of Jesus.

Twelve factors in Christology

At least twelve factors are involved when Jesus is interpreted. We say 'at least' because others may wish to add to them. And we call them 'factors in Christology', even though some who interpret Jesus are not undertaking the task of interpreting Jesus *for Christology* at all (i.e. they may not be interested in supporting the claim that Jesus is the Christ sent by God). Not all factors, in other words, are pertinent to all attempts to interpret Jesus. But when these factors are present, then Christology is being done. And the doing of Christology inevitably relates to, and sometimes incorporates, the work of those who do not operate in faith and for faith. The twelve factors are:

- historical
- philosophical (ontological)
- doctrinal

- doxological
- ecclesiastical
- communal (political)
- ethical
- experiential
- narrative
- biblical
- cultural
- eschatological.

The *historical* factor is one to which we have given a lot of space in this book. Historians are obviously concerned to know what Jesus of Nazareth was like. It is their job to find out. But, as we have seen, those who are influenced ethically by Jesus (whether they are Christian or not) need to know that Jesus was actually like the image they have of him. And those who interpret Jesus in theological terms always believe that it is *Jesus of Nazareth* they are interpreting, even if titles such as Saviour, Son of God and Lord also come into play. So most people will want to consider history when they are reading the Gospels.

We often imply, though, that history is somehow neutral, as if those who are ethically or theologically interested in Jesus are adding a further dimension to an otherwise neutral interest in Jesus. This is misleading. Historians are not *dis*interested, in the sense of being neutral. They try to be as clear as they can about 'the Jesus of history'. But though they focus on historical data, they may be serving lots of other interests too. For example, they might be writing an account of Jesus which by definition excludes the possibility of his undertaking any supernatural act, or showing how Jesus' words and actions place him in a tradition of thought which leads to Karl Marx, or even seeking to discredit Christian interpretations of Jesus. In none of these three cases need the other interest being served make them a bad historian. The philosophical, political and anti-doctrinal interests which we have just mentioned merely highlight the fact that history is not value-free. So no account of Jesus, and no reading of the Gospels, even that undertaken by historians, can be value-free.

The *philosophical* factor in Christology is therefore worth considering next. No one is without a philosophy. No one is without some basic assumptions about 'what we can know' (epistemology) or about 'the way things are' (ontology) even if these are rarely articulated. So when people interpret the figure of Jesus, they cannot but be affected by their most basic assumptions about human life. Examples of such basic assumptions include: how spirit and matter inter-relate; whether spirit can be seen as separate from matter at all; whether 'minds' exist;

whether a supreme mind (e.g. God) lies within or behind the universe. When Christians interpret Jesus, some of these assumptions will be more specific, such as whether Jesus, as Son of the Father, can still be 'really present' in people's lives. This clearly cannot mean that a first-century Palestinian figure from history is still with us. It therefore entails *ontological* assumptions. In Christology this means assumptions about who Jesus 'really was' and how the God who was present in the figure of Jesus can continue to be present in the same way today. Without such a philosophical factor at work, talk about any 'continuing presence of Jesus' is simply impossible.

When we speak of specifically Christian assumptions, though, we are entering the realm of theology and a range of factors come into play which only Christians would use explicitly. These are the *doctrinal*, the *doxological*, and the *ecclesiastical*.

The *doctrinal* factor refers to the issues we touched on when considering the 'canonical Jesus'. Jesus cannot be interpreted by Christians without reference to the history of interpretation to which the canonical Gospels gave rise. Taking doctrinal traditions seriously need not entail forcing the New Testament to mean something it cannot. Such could only be the conclusion of someone who believed Christianity to be wholly mistaken. It simply means that it is legitimate, even if the case still has to be argued, to see Christian doctrine as an extension of what the Gospels began to do, and to see the Gospels themselves as containing appropriate interpretations of the figure of Jesus. A space is thus preserved between history, biblical text and doctrinal history, so that mutual correction can continue to occur. But the possibility of continuity and coherence remains. There is, however, no escaping doctrinal traditions if one seeks to interpret Jesus within Christianity.

The *doxological* factor takes us in two directions. It acknowledges that God was worshipped in and through the figure of Jesus from an astonishingly early phase of Christianity's history. Therefore a long history of praise and worship of Jesus *as* God comes into play, even for the historian. For the Christian believer, there is also the fact that the worship of the Son, the second person of the Trinity, continues in the present. This cannot be permitted wholly to control what the interpreter of the Gospels finds in the texts. In the Gospels Jesus is simply not worshipped in the way that much contemporary Christian doxology implies. Equally, however, to ignore the praise of Jesus emerging within the Gospels would be to fail to do the Gospels justice. At the very least, respect for the doxological factor indicates that some interpreters of Jesus attach ultimate significance to the person they are interpreting. This makes the task of interpretation both important and dangerous: it must be done because the figure of Jesus matters so much; but when the person one is trying to interpret is also someone to be worshipped, then it is difficult to see how all the other factors can really carry anything like a comparative weight.

Thirdly, in this theological group of factors, there is the *ecclesiastical* factor, referring to the particular communities of faith to which Christian interpreters of the Gospels belong. We may therefore prefer to call this the 'denominational' or 'confessional' factor. No Christian interpreter can fail to be influenced by the particularity of their vision of God, church and world, as filtered through the body of believers to which they belong. There may be no such thing as a 'Baptist', a 'Roman Catholic' or a 'Methodist' Jesus. Such would be as objectionable as the Corinthians following Apollos or Cephas rather than Christ (1 Cor 1:12). But if we acknowledge that doctrine plays a part in our readings of the Gospels, and in our understandings of the figure of Jesus, then we cannot exclude the role played by the particular communities to which we belong.

Not all interpreters of Jesus belong to churches. But we must recognize that all interpretations of Jesus nevertheless locate their interpreters within particular communities. In this sense there is always a *communal* (or we may even say *political*) factor at work. The Marxist historian, for example, who wishes to claim Jesus as a proto-Marxist does so from within 'the Marxist community', however disparate and diverse that community may be. As we noted at the end of the first chapter of this book, no one reads in total isolation.

There are also other factors that need not be explicitly Christian, even while they may well take on Christian forms. These are the *ethical*, the *experiential*, the *narrative* and the *biblical*. We have dwelt already on the *ethical* influence of Jesus when considering his role as spiritual and ethical example in the previous chapter. Jesus plays this role for a wide range of people, not just Christians. It is important to note, however, how easily it can be assumed that Jesus supports the way we have already chosen to act. He therefore supports our pacifism, or our righteous anger, our socialism, communism or political conservatism. To say, therefore, that Jesus is an ethical influence is by no means to say enough. The content of that influence has yet to be determined. This is precisely where so many of the other factors become relevant. What we actually say about Jesus (and why) will determine the way in which he becomes an ethical influence.

The *experiential* factor of Jesus has two forms. For Christians it will probably include a sense of Jesus' 'continuing presence' (however that is understood). Christians are almost certain to speak of an 'experience of Jesus Christ' which will inform their reading of the Gospels. They will link it especially with the meaning of the resurrection stories from the Gospels, and the exploration of the doctrine of the Spirit in the New Testament. As we saw with Nick Cave, however, it is not only in that form that an experiential link is made with the figure of Jesus. Religious faith of a particular kind is not a requirement of an experiential, existential link existing between a Gospel reader and the figure of Jesus, even if specific forms of that link inevitably take shape within Christianity.

A *narrative* factor also relates to Christology. People enjoy hearing and telling stories, and the story of Jesus is endlessly fascinating because it is so rich and multi-faceted. Just as we create a narrative of our own life by the way we 'tell our own story', so we do the same with the story of Jesus. For whatever reason we tell his story (i.e. depending on which of the other factors are most dominant for us), we add to the fund of stories by, in effect, telling our own version of it and selecting our own extracts from the Gospels. And because a narrative form is clearly the most compelling way to tell the story of Jesus, creativity is positively involved. We are likely to be enthralled by creative re-tellings of the Gospels, and perhaps even to venture some of our own. Crossan's books on Jesus have sold well, not only because of their historical research, controversial conclusions and a good marketing strategy. He also happens to tell a very good tale.

The tenth factor to be considered is the *biblical*. It may seem surprising, in such a book as this, to be taking up this factor so late in the exposition. Yet there are many aspects of the biblical factor which need spelling out in the light of others. The biblical factor could easily be assumed to be fundamental. But Christology is about a person. The Christian Bible is but a means to the end of encountering a personal God, in and through the person of Jesus Christ. We have seen how the person of Jesus Christ is presented in many ways, even in the Gospels, let alone in the New Testament as a whole. What is more, little of the New Testament would be comprehensible without the Hebrew Bible, so both Testaments and the literature surrounding them give us important insights into who Jesus Christ was and is. From a theological perspective, the biblical factor picks up Martin Kähler's point, that Christology has to do with 'the biblical Christ' rather than 'the historical Jesus'. Even if debates will always go on as to how easily, if at all, the various New Testament witnesses can be unified or harmonized, it is theologically inevitable that some attempt is made to see what they have in common.

The biblical factor has a different dimension to it, however, for those who do not express an explicit theological interest. Historians, for example, have to make decisions as to what material they select from the available biblical texts. They must also decide whether the biblical or non-biblical sources may lead them to more reliable information about Jesus. This process in turn reminds the theologian that whatever the ecclesiastical significance of the various Christian canons may be, and whatever the church-related circumstances of their origin, use and contemporary authority, these canons are not the church's property. It is, indeed, precisely because the churches do not 'own' them that people are free to read them and make of them what they want. The figure of Jesus does indeed have an impact beyond both the printed word and beyond the churches which try to claim him for themselves.

A further factor, the *cultural*, offers this reminder in still starker form. 'Cultural' means anything that human beings create which helps them make sense of their world. Given the extent to which we now realize that we are all located within 'narratives' and 'cultures', it is not surprising we should consider Christology to have a 'cultural' aspect to it. Our use of the term here falls some way between the general use currently in vogue, and the more specific use of 'culture' as art. Acknowledging that there is a cultural factor in Christology is simply a way of accepting that *we* do the interpreting of Jesus, and that what we produce is not identical to the one we seek to interpret. The cultural factor is thus the narrative factor writ large. We may paint, write poems, compose music or make films about Jesus as a means of offering an interpretation. We may be affected by the poems, songs, hymns, oratorios, paintings and films produced by others. When we consider 'Jesus and the Gospels', we are, in fact, never just considering Jesus and the Gospels. Handel's *Messiah*, a painting by Rembrandt, a scene from Pasolini or Zeffirelli, may all affect our reading and our interpretation. It is unavoidable and can be fruitful. But, negatively expressed, it can also prevent us from allowing other factors to influence us.

Finally, we must mention the *eschatological* factor. This is not now the question of whether Jesus saw himself as an eschatological prophet. It is more to do with whether we can put up with not knowing; whether we can accept that of the making of many Jesuses there is no end; and that ultimately truth lies in the future. This factor functions methodologically as a summons to reticence and reserve about all our results. We must interpret Jesus Christ, for the figure of Jesus Christ is so important; but we dare not claim too much for our own particular version. That is the tension within which we all work and the reason why we have to remind ourselves that the future (and hence the ultimate meaning of Jesus Christ) is God's alone to give (1 Cor 13:12).

The twelve factors at work

All of these factors, then, interlock when Jesus is being interpreted as the Christ. Historians will explicitly relate to just some of them. Those who are influenced by Jesus, without professing any form of religious faith, will relate to a different selection. Christian believers will probably relate to most of them. Our point, in presenting this framework, has been to demonstrate how rich, diverse and vital the task presented by 'Jesus and the Gospels' actually is. The preceding chapters, though, have shown that some of these factors have not been given their due weight. We have sought, therefore, to relocate the study of 'Jesus and the Gospels' within this rich framework so that those who want to undertake theologically responsible study of the Gospels, in the service of Christology, may do so in an informed way. This conclusion should not, however, be understood to mean that this is the only way in which we believe the topic of 'Jesus and the Gospels' should be handled. We have sought to do justice to many interests in the figure of Jesus, and the different ways in which they influence the task of reading the Gospels.

The challenge of Jesus through the Gospels

As we have seen, the most well-known Gospels, those in the Christian Bible, are not just historical records. They remain influential texts within and beyond churches. They are interesting literature and are packed with good stories. They carry an authority by virtue of their proven track record. They speak of a compelling figure whose story and impact are complex and profound both within these texts themselves, and beyond. The challenge remains, therefore, to address the question of whether an adequate understanding of the figure of Jesus can only be gained when some form of Christology is undertaken. But that must be for the reader to judge, on the basis of their own Gospel reading, and by interacting with the twelve factors we have mapped out in this chapter.

Appendix

The earliest testimony to the Gospels is preserved in Eusebius's fourth-century work, *Historia Ecclesiae* (*H.E.*), now available as a Penguin paperback (*The History of the Church*, 1989). In the early part of this work, Eusebius records his own views about the Gospels. For example, he tells us that when Peter learnt that Mark had recorded his preaching, he was delighted and authorized its reading in the churches (2:15). He also claims that Mark was the first to carry the Christian message to Egypt (2:16). He thinks that Matthew, Mark and Luke all wrote about the final year of Jesus' life (after the Baptist was imprisoned), whereas John wrote about his early career, which explains (he thinks) the apparent discrepancies. And since Matthew and Luke include a genealogy and present Jesus as a man, John passed over this and began with the 'proclamation of His divinity since the Holy Spirit had reserved this for him, as the greatest of the four' (3:24).

But the significance of Eusebius's work is not so much his own conclusions as the fact that he includes quotations from Papias, Bishop of Hierapolis (*c.* 130 CE), Irenaeus, Bishop of Lyons (*c.* 180 CE), Clement of Alexandria (*c.* 200 CE) and Origen (*c.* 230 CE). These are our earliest witnesses to the authorship and character of the Gospels (two of Irenaeus's works are also extant). In the face of competing claims for other Gospels, Irenaeus argues that since there are four zones of the world, four principal winds, four cherubim and four covenants (Adam, Noah, Moses, Christ), it was fitting that God 'gave us the gospel under four forms but bound together by one Spirit' (Stevenson, 1957, p. 122). He also draws a parallel between the four living creatures of Revelation 4:7 (lion, ox, man, eagle) and the beginning of each of the Gospels (Burridge, 1994, pp. 1–32). The other important source comes from an eighth-century Latin manuscript known as the *Canon Muratori*, which is thought to be a translation of a third- or fourth-century Greek work. The fragment begins with the words 'at which he

was present and thus set them down', and then speaks about the origins
of Luke and John. It would appear that these were the concluding
words concerning Mark. The following extracts represent our main
sources for what the early church thought about the Gospels.

Matthew

Matthew compiled the *Sayings* in the Aramaic language, and everyone
translated them as well as he could. (Papias, *H.E.* 3:39)

Matthew published a written gospel for the Hebrews in their own
tongue, while Peter and Paul were preaching the gospel in Rome and
founding the church there. (Irenaeus, *H.E.* 5:8)

[The] third had the face as of a man – an evident description of His
advent as a human being... Matthew, again, relates His generation as a
man... This Gospel then is in human form; for which reason... the character of a humble and meek man is kept up through the whole Gospel.
(Irenaeus, 3:11.11; Stevenson, 1957, p. 122)

He [Clement of Alexandria] used to say that the earliest gospels were
those containing the genealogies. (*H.E.* 6:14)

First to be written was that of the one-time exciseman who became an
apostle of Jesus Christ – Matthew; it was published for believers of
Jewish origin, and was composed in Aramaic. (Origen, *H.E.* 6:25.7)

Mark

Mark, who had been Peter's interpreter, wrote down carefully, but not
in order, all that he remembered of the Lord's sayings and doings. For
he had not heard the Lord or been one of His followers, but later, as I
said, one of Peter's. Peter used to adapt his teachings to the occasion,
without making a systematic arrangement of the Lord's sayings, so that
Mark was quite justified in writing down some things just as he remembered them. For he had one purpose only – to leave out nothing that he
had heard, and to make no misstatement about it. (Papias, *H.E.* 3:39)

Mark also, the disciple and interpreter of Peter, transmitted to us in
writing the things preached by Peter. (Irenaeus, *H.E.* 5:8)

[The] fourth was like a flying eagle, pointing out the gift of the Spirit hov-
ering with His wings over the church... Mark... commences with the

prophetical spirit coming down from on high to men... pointing to the winged form of the Gospel; and on this account he made a compendious and cursory narrative, for such is the prophetical character. (Irenaeus, 3:11.11; Stevenson, 1957, p. 122)

When, at Rome, Peter had openly preached the word and by the spirit had proclaimed the gospel, the large audience urged Mark, who had followed him for a long time and remembered what had been said, to write it all down. This he did, making his gospel available to all who wanted it. When Peter heard about this, he made no objection and gave no special encouragement. (Clement of Alexandria, *H.E.* 6:14)

Next came that of Mark, who followed Peter's instructions in writing it, and who in Peter's general epistle was acknowledged as his son: 'Greetings to you from the church in Babylon, chosen like yourselves, and from my son Mark.' (Origen, *H.E.* 6:25.7)

Luke

Luke, the follower of Paul, set down in a book the gospel preached by him. (Irenaeus, *H.E.* 5:8)

[The] second was like a calf, signifying His sacrificial and sacerdotal order... Luke, taking up His priestly character, commenced with Zacharias the priest offering sacrifice to God. For now was made ready the fatted calf, about to be immolated for the finding again of the younger son. (Irenaeus, 3:11.11; Stevenson, 1957, p. 122)

Next came that of Luke, who wrote for Gentile converts the gospel praised by Paul. (Origen, *H.E.* 6:25.7)

The third book of the Gospel is that according to Luke. Luke, the physician, when, after the Ascension of Christ, Paul had taken him to himself as one studious of right [*or, probably,* as travelling companion] wrote in his own name what he had been told [*or* in order], although he had not himself seen the Lord in the flesh. He set down the events as far as he could ascertain them, and began his story with the birth of John. (*Canon Muratori*, Bettenson, 1969, p. 28)

John

John, the disciple of the Lord, who had leant back on His breast, once more set forth the gospel, while residing at Ephesus in Asia. (Irenaeus,

H.E. 5:8)

The first living creature was like a lion, symbolizing His effectual working, His supremacy and royal power... John relates His supreme, effectual, and glorious generation from the Father... For this reason, too, is that Gospel full of all confidence, for such is His person. (Irenaeus, 3:11.11; Stevenson, 1957, p. 122)

Last of all, aware that the physical facts had been recorded in the gospels, encouraged by his pupils and irresistibly moved by the Spirit, John wrote a spiritual gospel. (Clement of Alexandria, *H.E.* 6:14)

Need I say anything about the man who leant back on Jesus' breast, John? He left a single gospel, though he confessed that he could write so many that the whole world would not hold them. He also wrote the Revelation... In addition, he left an epistle of a very few lines, and possibly two more, though their authenticity is denied by some. (Origen, *H.E.* 6:25.7)

The fourth gospel is that of John, one of the disciples... When his fellow-disciples and bishops exhorted him he said, 'Fast with me for three days from to-day, and then let us relate to each other whatever may be revealed to each of us.' On the same night it was revealed to Andrew, one of the Apostles, that John should narrate all things in his own name as they remembered them. (*Canon Muratori*, Bettenson, 1969, p. 28)

Further reading

In order to further explore the Gospels, a good place to start is the Cambridge *New Testament Theology* Series (edited by J.D.G. Dunn). The individual volumes are written by U. Luz (Matthew, 1995), J.B. Green (Luke, 1995) and D. Moody Smith (John, 1995). For Mark, see J. Kingsbury's *The Christology of Mark* (1983) or W.R. Telford's Sheffield Guide *Mark* (1995). For more detailed work on the origins of the Gospels (including the apocryphal gospels), see *Ancient Christian Gospels: Their History and Development* (Koester, 1990) or *The Historical Jesus* (G. Theissen and A. Merz, 1998).

Both E.P. Sanders and J.D. Crossan have written major texts on the historical Jesus but a good place to begin is with their slimmer volumes. Sanders has contributed *The Historical Figure of Jesus* (1993) to the Penguin series and Crossan's *Jesus: A Revolutionary Biography* (1994) is a good way into his thought. See also Tom Wright's *The Victory of God* (1996).

For a theological appropriation of the Gospels, the Roman Catholic scholar Gerald O'Collins has written an excellent book, *Christology: A Biblical, Historical, and Systematic Study of Jesus* (1995). After summarizing the New Testament evidence, he looks at the developments that led to the creeds, issues that have been raised since then and his own proposal for a modern Christology. From the Protestant side, see J. Macquarrie's *Jesus Christ in Modern Thought* (1990) or J. Moltmann's *The Way of Jesus Christ* (1990).

Bibliography

Aichele, G., *Jesus Framed* (London/New York: Routledge, 1996).

Allison, D.C., *The New Moses: A Matthean Typology* (Minneapolis: Augsburg Fortress, 1993).

Bacon, B.S., *Studies in Matthew* (London: Constable, 1930).

Bauckham, R.A., (ed.) *The Gospels for All Christians* (Edinburgh: T & T Clark/Grand Rapids: Eerdmans, 1998).

Bettenson, H. (ed.), *Documents of the Christian Church* (2nd edn; Oxford/New York: Oxford University Press, 1963).

Bockmuehl, M., *This Jesus: Martyr, Lord, Messiah* (Edinburgh: T & T Clark, 1994).

Böll, H., *Mein Lesebuch* (Frankfurt am Main: Fischer Taschenbuch Verlag, 1978).

Borg, M.J., *Conflict, Holiness and Politics in the Teachings of Jesus* (New York/Toronto: The Edwin Mellen Press; rev. edn: Philadelphia: Trinity Press International, 1998 [1984]).

Borg, M.J., *Jesus: A New Vision* (San Francisco: Harper and Row/London: SPCK, 1987).

Borg, M.J., *Jesus in Contemporary Scholarship* (Valley Forge: Trinity Press International, 1994a).

Borg, M.J., *Meeting Jesus Again for the First Time* (San Francisco: HarperSanFrancisco, 1994b).

Borg, M.J., *The God We Never Knew: Beyond Dogmatic Religion to a More Authentic Contemporary Faith* (San Francisco: HarperSanFrancisco, 1997)

Borg, M.J. and Wright, N.T., *The Meaning of Jesus: Two Visions* (New York: HarperSanFrancisco, 1998).

Bultmann, R., *The Gospel of John: A Commentary* (Oxford: Blackwell, 1971).

Burridge, R.A., *Four Gospels, One Jesus?* (London: SPCK, 1994).

Casey, P.M., *From Jewish Prophet to Gentile God* (Cambridge: James Clarke, 1991).

Cave, N., *Introduction to the gospel according to mark* (Edinburgh: Canongate, 1998).

Chilton, B., (ed.) *The Kingdom of God* (London: SPCK/Philadelphia: Fortress Press, 1984).

Conzelmann, H., *The Theology of Saint Luke* (London: Faber/New York: Harper, 1960).

Cranfield, C.E.B., *The Gospel According to Saint Mark* (Cambridge: Cambridge University Press, 1959).

Creed, J.M., *The Gospel According to St Luke* (London: Macmillan, 1957).

Crossan, J.D., *The Cross that Spoke: The Origins of the Passion Narrative* (San Francisco: Harper and Row, 1988).

Crossan, J.D., *The Historical Jesus: The Life of a Mediterranean Jewish Peasant* (San Francisco: Harper Collins/Edinburgh: T & T Clark, 1991).

Crossan, J.D., *Jesus: A Revolutionary Biography* (San Francisco: HarperSanFrancisco, 1994).

Dodd, C.H., *The Parables of the Kingdom* (rev. edn: London: James Nisbet; reprinted as Fount paperback, 1978 [1961]).

Dodd, C.H., *Historical Tradition in the Fourth Gospel* (Cambridge, London, New York and Melbourne: Cambridge University Press, 1963).

Elliott, J.K., *The Apocryphal New Testament* (Oxford: Clarendon Press, 1993).

Evans, C.F., *Saint Luke* (London: SCM/Philadelphia: Trinity Press International, 1990).

Farmer, W.R., *The Synoptic Problem: A Critical Analysis* (London: Macmillan, 1964).

France, R.T., *Matthew – Evangelist and Teacher* (Exeter: Paternoster Press, 1989).

Freyne, S., *Galilee, Jesus and the Gospels: Literary Approaches and Historical Investigations* (Philadelphia: Fortress Press/Dublin: Gill and Macmillan, 1988).

Freyne, S., 'The Geography, Politics, and Economics of Galilee and the Quest for the Historical Jesus' in B. Chilton and C.A. Evans (eds) *Studying the Historical Jesus: Evaluations of the State of Current Research* (Leiden: Brill, 1994), pp. 75–121.

Funk, R.W. and Hoover, R.W., (eds) *The Five Gospels: The Search for the Authentic Words of Jesus* (New York: Polebridge Press, 1993).

Funk, R.W., (ed) *The Acts of Jesus* (San Francisco: HarperSanFrancisco, 1997).

Garrett, S.R., *The Temptations of Jesus in Mark's Gospel* (Grand Rapids/Cambridge: Eerdmans, 1998).

Goulder, M.D., *Luke: A New Paradigm* (Sheffield: JSOT Press, 1989).

Grant, R.M. and Freedman, D.N., *The Secret Sayings Of Jesus* (Garden City: Doubleday, 1960).

Green, J.B., *The Theology of the Gospel of Luke* (Cambridge: Cambridge University Press, 1995).

Gundry, R., *Mark: A Commentary on His Apology for the Cross* (Grand Rapids: Eerdmans, 1993).

Gundry, R., *Matthew: A Commentary on His Handbook for a Mixed Church under Persecution* (Grand Rapids: Eerdmans, 2nd edn, 1994).

Holtzmann, H.J., *Die synoptischen Evangelien* (1863 [never translated]).

Hooker, M.D., *The Son of Man in Mark* (London: SPCK, 1967).

Horsley, R.A., *Jesus and the Spiral of Violence* (San Francisco: Harper and Row, 1987).

Horsley, R.A., 'The Death of Jesus' in B. Chilton and C.A. Evans (eds) *Studying the Historical Jesus: Evaluations of the State of Current Research* (Leiden: Brill, 1994), pp. 395–422.

Jeremias, J., *The Parables of Jesus* (London: SCM 1972).

Jülicher, A., *Die Gleichnisreden Jesu* (1899 [never translated]).

Kähler, M., *The So-Called Historical Jesus and the Historic, Biblical Christ* (trans. C.E. Braaten; Philadelphia: Fortress Press, 1964 [1892]).

Käsemann, E., *The Testament of Jesus* (London: SCM, 1968).

Kingsbury, J.D., *The Christology of Mark's Gospel* (Philadelphia: Fortress Press, 1983).

Kingsbury, J.D., *Matthew As Story* (2nd edn; Philadelphia: Fortress Press, 1988).

Kloppenborg, J.S., *The Formation of Q: Trajectories in Ancient Wisdom Collections* (Philadelphia: Fortress Press, 1987).

Koester, H., *Ancient Christian Gospels: Their History and Development* (London: SCM/Philadelphia: Trinity Press International, 1990).

Lachman, C., 'De ordine narrationum in evangeliis synopticis' (1835 [never translated]).

Lightfoot, R.H., *The Gospel Message of St. Mark* (Oxford: Oxford University Press, 1950).

Luz, U., *The Theology of the Gospel of Matthew* (Cambridge: Cambridge University Press, 1995).

Mack, B.L., *A Myth of Innocence: Mark and Christian Origins* (Philadelphia: Fortress Press, 1988).

Mack, B.L., 'Q and a Cynic-Like Jesus' in *Whose Historical Jesus?* (eds W.E. Arnal & M. Desjardins; Ontario: Wilfrid Laurier University Press, 1997), pp. 25–36.

Macquarrie, J., *Jesus Christ in Modern Thought* (London: SCM, 1990).

Marcus, J., *The Way of the Lord: Christological Exegesis of the Old Testament in the Gospel of Mark* (Edinburgh: T & T Clark/Louisville: Westminster John Knox Press, 1992).

Meier, J.P., *A Marginal Jew: Rethinking the Historical Jesus*. Vol 1. *The Roots of the Problem and the Person* (New York: Doubleday, 1991).

Meier, J.P., *A Marginal Jew: Rethinking the Historical Jesus*. Vol 2. *Mentor, Message, and Miracles* (New York: Doubleday, 1994).

Miller, J.W., *Jesus at Thirty* (Philadelphia: Fortress Press, 1997).

Moltmann, J., *The Crucified God* (London: SCM, 1974).

Moltmann, J., *The Way of Jesus Christ* (London: SCM, 1990).

Moody Smith, D., *The Theology of the Gospel of John* (Cambridge: Cambridge University Press, 1995).

Moyise, S., *Introduction to Biblical Studies* (London: Cassell, 1998)

Nineham, D.E., *Saint Mark* (London: Penguin Books, 1963).

Nolland, J., *Luke 1–9:20* (WBC 35a; Dallas: Word Books, 1989).

Oakman, D.E., *Jesus and the Economic Questions of His Day* (Lewiston/Queenston: The Edwin Mellen Press, 1986).

O'Collins, G., *Christology: A Biblical, Historical, and Systematic Study of Jesus* (Oxford/New York: Oxford University Press, 1995).

Pelikan, J., *Jesus Through the Centuries* (New Haven and London: Yale University Press, 1985).

Powell, Mark Allan, *Fortress Introduction to the Gospels* (Minneapolis: Fortress Press, 1998).

Riches, J., *The World of Jesus: First Century Judaism in Crisis* (Cambridge: Cambridge University Press, 1990).

Riches, J., *Matthew* (NT Guides; Sheffield: Sheffield Academic Press, 1996).

Robinson, J.A.T., *The Priority of John* (London: SCM, 1985).

Sanders, E.P., *Jesus and Judaism* (London: SCM/Philadelphia: Fortress Press, 1985).

Sanders, E.P., *The Historical Figure of Jesus* (London: Penguin Books, 1993).

Schnackenburg, R., *Jesus in the Gospels. A Biblical Christology* (Louisville: Westminster John Knox Press, 1995).

Schüssler Fiorenza, E., *In Memory of Her: A Feminist Theological Reconstruction of Christian Origins* (London: SCM, 1983; rev. edn 1994).

Schweitzer, A., *The Quest of the Historical Jesus* (London: A & C Black, 3rd edn, 1954).

Sobrino, J., *Christology at the Crossroads* (London: SCM, 1978).

Stendahl, K., *The School of Matthew and its Use of the Old Testament* (2nd edn; Philadelphia: Fortress Press, 1968).

Stevenson, J. (ed.), *A New Eusebius* (London: SPCK, 1957).

Talbert, C.H., *Reading Luke* (London: SPCK/New York: Crossroad, 1982).

Taylor, V., *The Gospel According to Saint Mark* (London: Macmillan, 1952).

Telford, W.R., *Mark* (NT Guides; Sheffield: Sheffield Academic Press, 1995).

Theissen, G. and Merz, A., *The Historical Jesus* (London: SCM, 1998).

Thomson, M., 'The Historical Jesus and the Johannine Christ' in *Exploring the Gospel of John: In Honor of D. Moody Smith* (eds R.A.

Culpepper & C.C. Black; Louisville: John Knox Press, 1996), pp. 21–42.

Tuckett, C.M., *Luke* (NT Guides; Sheffield: Sheffield Academic Press, 1996).

Twelftree, G., *Jesus the Exorcist: A Contribution to the Study of the Historical Jesus* (WUNT 2.54; Tübingen: Mohr Siebeck, 1993 = Peabody: Hendrickson, 1994).

Vermes, G., *Jesus the Jew: A Historian's Reading of the Gospels* (London: SCM, 1973).

Vermes, G., *Jesus and the World of Judaism* (London: SCM, 1983).

Vermes, G., *The Religion of Jesus the Jew* (London: SCM, 1993).

Weiss, J., *Jesus' Proclamation of the Kingdom of God* (London: SCM/Philadelphia: Fortress Press; reprinted by Scholars Press 1985 [1971]).

Witherington, B., *Jesus the Sage: The Pilgrimage of Wisdom* (Minneapolis: Fortress Press, 1994).

Wrede, W., *The Messianic Secret* (Cambridge: James Clarke, 1971 [1901]).

Wright, N.T., *Christian Origins and the Question of God* Vol 1: *The New Testament and the People of God* (London: SPCK/Minneapolis: Fortress Press, 1992).

Wright, N.T., *Christian Origins and the Question of God* Vol 2: *Jesus and the Victory of God* (London: SPCK, 1996).

Index

Aichele, G. 25
Allison. D.C. 31
anti-Semitism 36–7, 94
apocalyptic 18, 27, 38, 43, 47, 58, 76-86, 89-91, 98
apocryphal gospels 63–71, 119
authorship of the gospels 22, 29–30, 36, 39-40, 51, 115–18
baptism of Jesus 14, 22, 52–3, 64, 76
Bacon, B.S. 30, 36
basileia 11–12, 99–101
Bauckham, R.A. 15, 60
Bettenson, H. 117–18
Bockmuehl, M. 105
Böll, H. 101–2
Borg, M.J. 88–9, 92–5
Bultmann, R. 54–5
Burridge, R. 9, 46, 115

canon 63, 67, 71–2, 104–7, 115
Casey, P.M. 59
Cave, N. 102–3, 112
Chilton, B. 94
Clement of Alexandria 60, 115–18
Conzelmann, H. 47–8
Cranfield, C.E.B. 21, 23
Creed, J.M., 45
Crossan, J.D. 67, 84–8, 92–4, 119
crucifixion 15, 20–2, 35, 46–7, 59, 66–8, 73, 98

Cynicism 31, 84–9

Dead Sea Scrolls 29, 52, 71
divinity of Christ 57, 87, 115
docetism 12, 59–60
Dodd, C.H. 90–5

Elliott, J.K. 67, 69
eschatology 10–11, 18, 47–8, 58, 72–83, 89–93
eucharist 41, 53, 55
Evans, C.F. 42

Farmer, W.R. 25
feminist theology 11, 99–101
form criticism 12–13, 72, 78
France, R.T. 30
Freyne, S. 11, 83
Funk, R.W. 66

Garrett, S.R. 19
genealogy of Jesus 27, 40, 47, 115
Gethsemane 15, 20–1, 44, 55
Goulder, M.D. 38
Grant, R.M. 63
Green, J.B. 46, 119
Gundry, R. 16, 22, 32

historical criticism 7–10, 12–13, 59–63, 71, 78, 81, 97, 100, 103, 107, 109

Holtzmann, H.J. 14
Hooker, M.D. 25
Hoover, R.W. 66
Horsley, R.A. 11, 83–4
humanity of Jesus 12, 38–9, 46, 102

infancy stories 27–30, 39–40, 69–71

Jeremias, J. 64
Jesus Seminar 39, 92
John the Baptist 15, 52–3, 78, 81, 85, 99
Jülicher, A. 63

Kähler, M. 104, 112
Käsemann, E. 59
kingdom of God 11, 17–19, 23, 25–6, 35, 37, 47–8, 58, 65, 67, 73–83, 85–9, 97–101
Kingsbury, J.D. 19, 35, 119
Kloppenborg, J.S. 66
Koester, H. 64–6, 119

Lachman, C. 14
liberator, Jesus as 11, 96–9
Lightfoot, R.H. 14
lord, Jesus as 48
Luz, U. 32–3, 119

Mack, B.L. 31, 67
Macquarrie, J. 119
Marcus, J. 21
Meier, J.P. 12
messiah, Jesus as 7, 23–4, 27–8, 35, 48, 52, 57–8, 87, 90–2
Miller, J.W. 88
miracles of Jesus 12, 16–17, 19–23, 26, 33–4, 46, 53–4, 70, 76, 79, 87, 90
Moltmann, J. 25, 119
Moody Smith, D. 58, 119
Moyise, S. 12

Nineham, D.E. 22
Nolland, J. 40

Oakman, D.E. 11, 84
O'Collins, G. 119

parables of Jesus 17, 33, 38, 46, 51, 63–4, 91
Pelikan, J. 9
Powell, M.A. 35
prophet, Jesus as 10–11, 15, 42, 45–6, 49, 59, 64, 72–83, 88, 92–3
Protoevangelium of James 69–71
Pseudo-Matthew, Gospel of 69–71

Q 31, 38, 42, 48, 65–7, 86, 94, 100

realized eschatology 91–2
redaction criticism 12–13, 66, 108
resurrection stories 15, 25, 27, 32, 40–1, 56, 68, 105
Riches, J. 34–5, 81
Robinson, J.A.T. 60

Sanders, E.P. 36, 66, 75–83, 89–90, 119
saviour, Jesus as 8, 47–8, 68, 102, 109
Schnackenburg, R. 35, 36, 61
Schüssler Fiorenza, E., 11, 99–101
Schweitzer, A. 18, 72–83, 89, 94
Sobrino, J. 11, 96–9
son of God 7, 19, 22–5, 27, 32, 35, 37, 55, 57–62, 79, 109
son of man 16–18, 21, 23–5, 33, 44, 64, 66, 79
Stendahl, K. 29
Stevenson, J. 116–18

Talbert, C.H. 41, 44
Taylor, V. 21
Telford, W.R. 119
Theissen, G. 12, 16, 67, 119

Thomas, Gospel of 7, 63–7, 85, 88,
  93–4, 103
Thomson, M. 61
Tuckett, C.M. 47
Twelftree, G. 12

Vermes, G. 83

Weiss, J. 73–83
wisdom, Jesus as 52
Withérington, B. 11
Wrede, W. 23, 72, 90–5
Wright, N.T. 10–11, 46, 48, 81–2,
  89–90, 95, 119